China 1968: peasants welcoming a poster of Liu Chunhua's Chairman Mao
goes to An-yuan. *About 900 million posters were printed and sold, and the
image was also issued as a postage stamp*

INDEX ON CENSORSHIP 1 1997

Volume 26 No 1 January/February 1997 Issue 174

Australian committee Philip Adams, Blanche d'Alpuget, Bruce Dawe, Adele Horin, Angelo Loukakis, Ken Methold, Laurie Muller, Robert Pullan and David Williamson c/o Ken Methold, PO Box 825, Glebe NSW 2037, Australia

Danish committee Paul Grosen, Niels Barfoed, Claus Sønderkøge, Herbert Pundik, Nils Thostrup, Toni Liversage and Björn Elmquist, c/o Claus Sønderkøge, Utkaervej 7, Ejerslev, DK-7900 Nykobing Mors, Denmark

Dutch committee Maarten Asscher, Gerlien van Dalen, Christel Jansen, Chris Keulemans, Wieke Rombach, Mineke Schipper and Steven de Winter, c/o Gerlien van Dalen and Chris Keulemans, De Balie, Kleine-Gartmanplantsoen 10, 1017 RR Amsterdam

Norwegian committee Trond Andreassen, Jahn Otto Johansen, Alf Skjeseth and Sigmund Strømme, c/o NFF, Bydøy allé 21, N-0262 Oslo, Norway

Swedish committee Gunilla Abrandt and Ana L Valdés, c/o Dagens Nyheter, Kulturredaktionen, S-105 15 Stockholm, Sweden

USA committee Ariel Dorfman, Rea Hederman, Peter Jennings, Harvey J Kaye, Susan Kenny, Jane Kramer, Radha Kumar, Jeri Laber, Gara LaMarche, Anne Nelson, Faith Sale, Gaye Salisbury, Michael Scammell, Vivienne Walt

Cover illustrations
Front cover Liu Chunhua 'Chairman Mao Goes to An-yuan' 1995/Hanart TZ Gallery Hong Kong *Back cover* Illustrations by Huang Yongyu from *Animal Antics*
Main illustration 'Laughter': 'The 15-minute interval between two tearful performances' 'Balloon': 'Big and bright and a high-flyer easily deflated by the least criticism'

Former Editors: Michael Scammell (1972-81); Hugh Lunghi (1981-83); George Theiner (1983-88); Sally Laird (1988-89); Andrew Graham-Yooll (1989-93)

EDITORIAL

Two-way drift

'ROLL ON 1997/Then I'll be able to go to Hong Kong' sang the Shenyang singer Ai Jing in Beijing as long ago as 1991. On 1 July 1997, Hong Kong, after a century and a half of British rule, returns to the People's Republic of China and *Index*, in a comprehensive and in-depth report, looks at exactly why it matters and how it will affect both sides of the equation.

On China's present record, the prospect for freedom of expression and human rights in Hong Kong is not a happy one, as our report repeatedly demonstrates.

And yet the story is more complicated. China's foremost academic in exile, Liu Binyan, says the Chinese government, despite relentless political repression since 1989, is 'steadily more anxious about political and social stability': China's Central Propaganda Department has admitted to over 10,000 demonstrations and protests in urban and rural areas over the past year. And as Geremie Barmé says, Hong Kong — 'with its hip, modernised Shanghai decadence' — has been importing new ideas and new lifestyles into China for over a decade.

Few Hong Kong residents deny their Chinese ancestry, but their cultural identification by no means implies unquestioned political commitment. If it comes to outright confrontation, the giant will always win. But though many of our contributors see no grounds for optimism, others argue that at the level of cultural seepage and glimpses of new expressive possibilities — in film, music, language, alternative mores — Hong Kong's imports have been shaping the face of the mainland for some time.

Such infiltration is a slow, long-term project. Meanwhile, the most draconian censorship regime in China since the Cultural Revolution is giving the people of Hong Kong a crash course in what might be in store for them.

YOU'LL be hearing from us throughout 1997, because this is *Index*'s twenty-fifth birthday year. We have the film première of Arthur Miller's *The Crucible* in February, a special anniversary issue of *Index* in May, the publication of an anthology of the best of *Index* (Gollancz) and two readers, *Film and Censorship* and *From Communism to Nationalism* (Cassell), the first Stephen Spender Memorial readings in Britain and the US, and *Index* events at a number of literary festivals. Celebrate the year with us. ❏

contents

Index on Censorship **and**
Writers and Scholars Educational Trust

depend on donations to guarantee their independence and to fund research
The Trustees and Directors would like to thank all those whose
donations support Index and WSET, including

The Bromley Trust
Drue Heinz Foundation
The European Commission
The Paul Hamlyn Foundation
The Ministry of Foreign Affairs, the Netherlands
The Onaway Trust
The Royal Danish Ministry of Foreign Affairs
Time Inc

- **No more bans** Film censorship in Denmark was banned on 1 January. 'It's the job of parents, not of the state to be responsible for what their children watch,' said culture minister Jyette Hilden.

- **China's battered wives** are getting bolder. In 1991, they lodged 638 complaints with Guangzhou Women's Federation; in 1994, 2,567 came forward; and in 1995 their ranks had swollen to 2,830.

- **Virtual wars** China's first cyber opposition movement has mobilised round the Diaoyu Islands issue. Heated polemic on the government's pusillanimous attitude over the Islands poured into the website at Funan University in Shanghai. Traffic was terminated by the authorities because it was jamming the university's computers.

- **Dirty shirts** New Zealand's censorship board reports that it examined a total of 2,063 films, magazines, posters, and CD-Roms last year — plus one article of clothing. The item in question, a T-shirt depicting cartoon babies in sexual poses, was banned.

- **Down tools** Women of Colombia say no to bearing any more children until their men stop waging war.

- **Battle of the bulge** Sexual equality suffered a reverse blow when the UK's Advertising Standards Authority banned an ad for male underwear featuring a close-up of a well-endowed model blazoned with the slogan 'The Loin King'. If Wonderbra got away with their traffic-stopping ad featuring the ample bosom of Eva Herzigova, asks a representative of the manufacturer Brass Monkeys, why should we be asked to provide a 'smaller' model?

• **Morocco unbound** Antoine Gallimard, head of the French publishing house Gallimard, was unceremoniously expelled from Morocco in November after having been officially invited to attend the Casablanca Book Fair. No explanation was forthcoming: anxious not to make waves in a favoured ex-colony, the French Embassy in Rabat put it down to a 'bureaucratic muddle'. The victim himself, on the word of the same Embassy — but in private — attributed it to the publication by Gallimard in 1990 of Gilles Perrault's less than fulsome book on Morocco's ruler, *Our Friend the King*.

• **Better late than never** On election day in the USA a Federal Appeals Court ruled unconstitutional a government requirement that the federally funded National Endowment for the Arts apply 'general standards of decency and respect' in assessing grant requests. By a two-to-one vote, the court determined that 'even when the government is funding speech it may not distinguish between speakers on the basis of the speaker's viewpoint or otherwise aim at the suppression of dangerous ideas.'

• **Don't cry for me** The North Korean famine is getting worse, with this year's grain harvest badly hit by floods. As the Red Cross appeals in vain for extra help from the South, the government of Kim Chong-il has taken decisive action — by banning funerals for the under-60s. Crying is also prohibited. Families of under-age famine victims in Hamgyong and Yanggang provinces may only bury the bodies at night, or at sea. Said one local observer: 'People older than 60 are allowed to be given funerals. Perhaps this is because their deaths are considered to be unconnected to the food shortage.'

• **Costumeless drama** India's censors are balking at a film version of the *Kamasutra*, and are demanding cuts of all scenes of nudity. The film, directed by Mira Nair, has been critically acclaimed abroad as an exploration of female sexuality. The complicated rules of Indian film censorship allow depictions of sexual violence and women in wet-look saris, but draw the line at nudity and, until very recently, kissing.

• **Whom the gods would destroy** Meanwhile, one of the country's best-known artists, Maqbool

Husain, has got into trouble with Hindu activists for his unclothed representation of the goddess Saraswati. Militants of the Bajrang Dal stormed into Ahmedabad's Herwitz Gallery and destroyed several Husain canvases and tapestries in protest. Despite Hinduism's long tradition of nude deities, Husain has been charged (under legislation dating back to the Raj) of offending religious feelings. The real problem, of course, is Husain's own religion — he's a Muslim.

• **The agony and...** 'Britain Set for Court Defeat', 'Blasphemy Law Faces Last Judgement' yelled the headlines — but the European Court of Human Rights unexpectedly upheld the seven-year ban on the video *Visions of Ecstasy* in November, giving tacit backing to Britain's archaic blasphemy law into the bargain. The court ruled that questions of blasphemy should be decided at the national, not the European, level. Two judges dissented, on the basis that the ban is a clear case of prior restraint and that the need for a blasphemy law is 'very much open to question'. According to the film's director, Nigel Wingrove, 'Britain now has the heaviest censorship in the western world. I don't think that's anything for the government to be proud about.'

• **Not with a roar, more like a squeak** While Bill Clinton promoted free trade at November's Asia Pacific Economic Co-operation summit in the Philippines, and apparently deferred to Asian leaders by avoiding human rights issues, the Walt Disney Corporation resisted Chinese demands that it cease production of the film *Kundun*, based on the life of the Dalai Lama. Despite implied threats by the Chinese government to shelve Disney's plans for a projected theme park in China and to curtail the company's booming Chinese sales and investments — most notably the marketing of animated movies such as *The Lion King* and the Disney-owned retail operation 'Mickey's Corner' — Disney affirmed it was going ahead with the movie. But for how long? Disney President Steve Ovitz, the man responsible for telling China to get lost, has just resigned 'by mutual agreement'.

• **Timing is all** The BBC's World Service is to cut half its Cantonese-language service, saying that they only have a few listeners in Hong Kong and fewer still in southern China. It's all in the name of economy: the cash-straitened organisation has had its budget slashed by the government and is expected to make savings — while maintaining its reputation as a flagship news and current affairs service. Insiders are dubious about the purported lack of listeners and say that saving money is one thing; but cutting the broadcasts in April, just two months before the handover to China, is something else.

• **Net gain** Germany's Technology Ministry gave Internet Service Providers (ISPs) an unexpected boost by announcing that they will not be held liable for illegal material, such as child pornography, bomb-making manuals and neo-Nazi propaganda, on their systems, unless they are aware of its presence. This goes firmly against the trend in most of the world, which is to put as much pressure as possible on ISPs to take responsibility for controlling the spread of such material.

• **Safety net** While the rest of the world frets about how to regulate the Internet, the government of Laos — one of the few unreconstructed Communist countries on the planet — has banned it outright. Citing national security reasons, the government has announced hefty fines and threatened confiscation of equipment for anyone caught *in flagrante* — even though the country has no service providers whatsoever.

• **Net profit** Meanwhile, as the US Justice Department waits for the Supreme Court to begin deliberations on the fate of the Communications Decency Act, President Clinton is being advised of the economic potential in applying free-market policies in cyberspace. A leaked report from senior presidential advisers warns that attempts to control content on the Net could have serious commercial fallout. Online sales of goods and services are forecast to grow to US$7 billion by the century's end.

• **Bad to verse** President Lukashenka left Belarusian voters in no doubt as to how to cast their ballots in November's referendum. Each was handed a pre-marked specimen voting slip, with the helpful verse:

If you want order in our Republic
If you don't want trouble and row
Then at one, two, seven, cross out
'Against'
And elsewhere cross out 'For' —
that's how!

• **And the winner is...** The World Intellectual Property Organisation, a branch of the United Nations, awarded a Medal of Achievement to Nigeria's president, General Sani Abacha, almost a year to the day after the execution of Ken Saro-Wiwa and eight other Ogoni activists. Nigeria's Nobel laureate, Wole Soyinka, fulminated: 'What sickness is this that honours a vicious tyrant, a persecutor and destroyer of a nation's intellectual community, a media arsonist, a torturer and murderer of journalists, students, writers, musicians and academics, with a prestigious medal that should be the rare attribution of merit for those who espouse the cause of intellect... By this act, this man, this ghoul, Mr Bogsch, the head of WIPO, has openly mocked the death of Ken Saro-Wiwa and his companions, and danced on their graves. In anointing Ken Saro-Wiwa's murderer and trumpeting such obscenity to the world as a deed of merit, he forfeits the right to direct a body dedicated to the enhancement of the human mind and its strivings.' The WIPO declined to comment.

• **Cover-ups** With elections over and Christmas shopping commencing, politics gave way to campaigns and cover-ups of another kind. Finding 'Parental Advisory' labels insufficient warning, the 'family-oriented' 2,300-store Wal-Mart retail chain — the USA's largest single purveyor of pop music — has been demanding that record companies start producing 'clean' versions in which words are blanked out and pictures are altered. Artists and consumers protest that Wal-Mart's actions constitute censorship. Corporate spokespeople contend that shoppers can go elsewhere for the unexpurgated versions; although Wal-Mart's marketing prowess has already driven out the competition from many towns.

• **A Dublin crime reporter** was nearly jailed for refusing to name his sources of information in a civil trial in which he was a witness. Barry O'Kelly, now with the *Star*, wrote the offending story for the *Irish Press* two years ago. However, before being jailed his lawyers argued that clarification was necessary: either the law has evolved since the broadcast journalist Kevin O'Kelly was jailed in the early 1970s, granting a de facto protection to sources, they said; or, Irish law is in breach of the European Convention on Human Rights, following the case of *Goodwin v UK* last year. Following the much-publicised case of Susan O'Keeffe, a journalist with the British television programme *World In Action* who in 1992 refused to name her sources to a tribunal of inquiry into the beef industry, the government promised action on the question of journalists being charged with contempt of court for guarding their sources. But O'Keeffe's release on a technicality, without naming her sources, meant that the government did nothing about the law. The O'Kelly case is expected to be of major significance for Irish media law and could itself end up in the European Court of Human Rights. Both the National Union of Journalists and the *Star* have promised to fund a case.

• **A bad rap** In an unprecedented judgement, Kool Shen and Joey Starr of France's leading rap group NTM (Nique Ta Mère/Fuck Your Mother), were condemned by a Toulon court in November to three months' imprisonment, a six-month ban on performing and a fine of FF50,000 (US$10,000) for 'verbal abuse of the police'. The case was brought by local law enforcement officials responsible for security at a 'Concert for Freedom' staged to protest against the victory of the National Front in Toulon. 'Bugger justice, piss on it. Police are fascists, they're the ones who murder. Where's the law and those buggers in blue who shit on us year round? The fascists aren't just in Toulon: they travel in threes in their blues in a Renault 19...' and so on.

Politicians, unions, youth and student organisations as well as anti-racist groups protested the sentence. Yet *Le Monde*'s editorialist could ask on 18 November, 'Have our politicians no idea what's going on in the suburbs? Rap is the music of the oppressed, the sound of the ghetto... that evokes the grief and despair of minorities, racism, urban violence, drugs, etc... Neither the judge in

Toulon, nor those many politicians who have approved the sentence seem to have the least notion of the message of incomprehension they are giving to a lost generation, perhaps even now at the point of revolt.'

As *Le Monde* feared, the fine words and the indignation were quickly forgotten and things returned to normal. The 'explosion' of which it warned has not happened. But not all the country's politicians are deaf to the sound of the ghetto. In December the speaker of the National Assembly, Philippe Séguin, called for a thorough investigation by party leaders after an unidentified MP shouted out 'nique ta mère' during question time.

• **Democracy postponed** In the second round of local elections in Serbia on 17 November, the opposition coalition Zajedno (Together) claimed landslide victories in 15 of Serbia's urban centres, including the capital Belgrade and the key cities Nis and Novi Sad. These unprecedented results followed the victory of ruling Socialist Party of Serbia (SPS) in federal elections only a week earlier. Analysts pointed out that, while few were willing to question the leadership of President Milosevic himself, many were tired of the policies and corruption of the local SPS chiefs.

The SPS proceeded to annul the results, citing a large number of unspecified electoral irregularities as justification. In Nis — a traditional

Socialist stronghold — the method for cancelling the results was particularly crude: the local electoral commission simply changed the number of votes for the respective parties in favour of the SPS. In Belgrade and other towns, votes were cancelled by local municipal court decisions and a third round of local elections was called. The opposition boycotted those elections, though some of their supporters voted nevertheless. Zajedno's election monitors reported that turnout was as low as 12-15 per cent.

Public protest at what opposition supporters called the high-handed and illegal theft of their votes by the ruling Socialists first began in Nis on 19 November. The protest quickly spread to other cities and as many as 150,000 turned out daily on the streets of Belgrade in the weeks that followed. The student protest began three days into the opposition-led demonstrations but remained autonomous of that opposition. They have their own demands: the resignation of the dean of the University of Belgrade; the resignation of the dean of students at the University; and the establishment of an all-party commission to examine the election results.

From the outset President Milosevic refused to give any public statement on the crisis and for the first two weeks barred his media from reporting the protests. The only media to cover the demonstrations were the independent ones, notably Radio B-92, Radio Index and Boom 93. Following week-long jamming of the frequencies of those three stations they were banned on 3 December. Only Radio Index and B-92 were allowed to resume broadcasting about 48 hours later. Boom 93, in Pozeravac — a provincial town 50 miles south of Belgrade and best known as the birthplace of Milosevic — remains closed.

State television broke its silence on the peaceful demonstrations on 1 December, when the president of the Serbian Parliament, Dragan Tomic, launched a vitriolic attack on the opposition and their supporters, likening the opposition to fascists and accusing them of manipulating children for political ends.

On 8 December the Supreme Court of Serbia turned down a number of complaints submitted jointly by Zajedno and the Belgrade electoral commission, the same electoral commission that cancelled opposition victories in Belgrade in the first place. On 10 December, the Federal Court also rejected the electoral commission's request to re-examine the decision of the Supreme Court. All legal means to resolve the conflict have now been exhausted.

• **In China**, signs of the race towards modernisation are everywhere. Fashions, technology, aspirations: all have changed dramatically in little more than a decade. Radio phone-in programmes discuss callers' problems; in a storm of computer-generated graphics, slick young presenters introduce pop music shows on TV. In the 'golden minute' — peak viewing time on national television — imported gold watches bask in the spotlight that has cost their advertisers millions of dollars. It's 7pm — here is the news: 'Prime Minister Li Peng has welcomed the head of a Bulgarian parliamentary delegation, reporters from the *People's Daily* have discovered a new revolutionary hero, a model soldier who has dedicated his whole life to serving the motherland.'

This is China in the late 1990s. A leadership fearful that amid all the changes, society is slipping from its grasp, is reverting to type. The airwaves reverberate with the leaden sound of Party ideologues trying to reimpose their will on the masses. President Jiang Zemin has been warning of the dangers of an ideological vacuum that could threaten the Communist Party's (and his own) legitimacy. His proposed solution only emphasises the generation gap between Party elders and the nation's youth — a campaign to promote 'Spiritual Civilisation'. Summed up in a 15,000-word tract hailed by the Party as one of its greatest documents ever, it consists of political education for officials and, for the public, a relentless 1950s-style campaign promoting hand-picked individuals as uplifting examples of patriotism and altruism.

The old vocabulary is back in vogue: a retired hairdresser from the Shenzhen special economic zone suddenly finds herself lauded as the living embodiment of Lei Feng, the selfless soldier who served as a useful icon in the 1960s and is now being invoked for a new generation. A Beijing bus conductress, a plumber from Shanghai, a Party official who died in Tibet: the official media is full of them. Plays have been written, films made, a new book entitled *Role Models Since the Founding of the Republic* is being rushed out.

The leadership's gamble is that this will instil the required patriotism and love for a Party that sees itself as the embodiment of the nation. Many in the cities now scoff at this kind of campaign, but in rural areas, and perhaps among the older generation, it may have more impact. The Party seems to hope that modern technology and images of China's might will impress the people. It makes for a sometimes incongruous mixture — witness the video of a pop song extolling the People's Liberation Army, in which glamorous women in stylishly cut military uniforms pout seductively alongside a battalion of rocket launchers.

The Spiritual Civilisation Campaign is being spearheaded by the Communist Party's man of the moment, propaganda chief Ding Guangen. The way he employs television, films, opera, and pop music to get the message across is a throwback to the Communist Party's long tradition of seeing the cultural sphere as just another arena of politics. For writers, artists and film-makers it's a worrying development, a sign that, in the vocabulary of Chinese cultural politics, a 'chill wind' is blowing again.

Ding and his colleagues evidently believe that the limited loosening of controls over the arts and the publishing sector have gone too far, and are contributing to declining moral standards. Many in China would agree that too many canny entrepreneurs have been cashing in on the booming market for pornographic magazines and books. But the Party's definition of pornography tends to include anything it considers politically unacceptable. Film-makers have been among the first to feel the sting of the latest campaign.

Meanwhile, foreign journalists have been criticised for failing to understand China and domestic newspaper editors have been sacked as Ding's campaign starts to bite. A commentary in the *People's Daily* accused writers of 'divorcing literature and the arts from reality and politics'; film-makers have been told they must move closer to the 'masses'; and several have been attacked in the press for pandering to foreign tastes. Figures who in the past have escaped relatively unscathed are now targets of criticism: Mo Yan, author of the novel *Red Sorghum* (basis for Zhang Yimou's first film), has been accused of salacious writing. And Wang Shuo, the *enfant terrible* of Chinese literature who has become a millionaire with his satirical tales of

modern youth, has had his latest film pulled in mid-production and his books withdrawn from bookshops.

As always in China, the boundaries are never completely clear and some artists will no doubt be untouched by the campaign. But it will only add to the pressure for self-censorship. And for those whose writing touches on the political — even if only in a theoretical way — the consequences are grave: the recent imprisonment of Wang Dan and Liu Xiaobo is a reminder of this. Chinese writers at least have some idea of the ground rules of the system, and to some extent are able to read between the lines of official pronouncements. It's a discipline in which the people of Hong Kong are likely soon to receive a crash course.

To President Ali Akhbar Hashemi Rafsanjani: WANTED! Information on the whereabouts of FARRAJ SARKOOHI, writer and editor, last seen on 12 November, boarding an Iran Air flight from Tehran to Hamburg where his wife and children were waiting for him.

Despite assurances from the Iranian government that he has left the country, Sarkoohi did not arrive in Germany and has not been heard of since. His family and friends in Iran and outside are concerned that he is being held in an unofficial detention centre, and may already be dead. In view of the fate of his colleague, writer and poet Ghaffar Hosseini, discovered dead from an unexplained heart attack on 11 November, we appeal to the Iranian government, or anyone with information, to reveal the whereabouts of Farraj Sarkoohi.

Sarkoohi and Hosseini — along with Ahmed Miralai who was found dead in a Tehran alley after having been interrogated by Iranian security officials in October 1995 — were signatories to the 1994 appeal from 134 Iranian writers calling for an end to censorship (*Index* 6/1994).

Along with Edward Albee, Gunter Grass, Eric Hobsbawm, Arthur Miller, Edward Saïd and Susan Sontag, all signatories of PEN's open letter to you, and with writers and journalists around the world, we warn you that we hold you responsible for the safety of Sarkoohi.

And then there is the case of photographer and film maker Kaveh Golestan, AP's accredited correspondent in Iran, and journalist Nabih Zare-Kamel, accused of 'treachery' for their part in a film, made with the approval of UNICEF, of the Hazrat Ali Asylum for mentally handicapped children in Tehran. You will be aware by now, President Hashemi Rafsanjani, that your local UNICEF policy director, Mohammed Reza Hosseini, has deceived yourself and UNICEF alike. In an attempt to cover up his own culpability, he is accusing Golestan of falsifying his film to discredit Iran, of 'treachery', 'Zionism' and spying for the USA. The horrifying scenes in the children's asylum must be laid at the door of negligent local UNICEF officials. It is they who are discrediting the Islamic Republic, not journalists seeking to expose the corruption that shames the state.

Under Iranian law, Golestan and Zare-Kamel face trial and imprisonment. You are said to be 'outraged' at the scenes in the film showing conditions in the asylum, and to have ordered an investigation. We ask you, with UNICEF, to get to the truth of this affair and to call off the press witch-hunt against Golestan before it is too late. ❏

South Bank, London 3 December 1996: (From left to right, seated) Doris Lessing, Liu Hongbin, Salman Rushdie; (standing) Ghazi Rabihavi, Nedim Gürsel and Alberto Manguel in the Purcell Room for an evening of readings from 'Lost Words', Index *6/1996*

ADEWALE MAJA-PEARCE

On the move again

Journalists jostle for pictures, aid agencies hawk their wares in competition one with another, and the UNHCR fortifies itself against the unexpected

I WAS standing within sight of the border post that the refugees had been crossing for the past three days at the rate of 10,000 an hour. Here was Africa on the move again, half a million in this case walking from Zaire back home to Rwanda, many of them without shoes, the children tethered to their parents by lengths of string lest they get lost in the crush of people, as in fact happened anyway. One of the aid workers said that the worst cases were those of children too young to give a name, any name, in which case all they could do was take a photograph and show it around, but this wasn't proving very successful. There were just too many people. And still they kept coming: the old couple holding hands, the man pushing his friend in a wheelchair, the woman cradling a day-old infant. A nurse with one of the aid agencies told me that he had attended four deliveries the previous day.

I had been in the town for five days now. I was planning to return to Kigali, the capital, the following day because there was nothing else to see except more refugees. I just wanted to take one last look at the border itself, in this case a long iron bar supported three feet above the ground at either end. This represented the magical line that separated two countries, two governments but, being Africa, very often the same tribe or ethnic group or whatever the preferred nomenclature. For the present, the iron bar had been removed in order to facilitate the movement of the refugees, who were nevertheless obliged by the strict and always professional Rwandan soldiers to pass between the two supports, which were placed about 12 feet apart.

To the right of the border, on the Rwandan side, a jeep belonging to

Zaire-Rwandan border, August 1994: today she is on the move once more

the United Nations High Commissioner for Refugees (UNHCR) was parked on a slight incline overlooking the red earth of the unpaved road that had been hammered hard and flat. A white man was leaning on the bonnet of the jeep writing something in a book. Perhaps he was the one whose job it was to count the number of refugees per hour. Across from him, on the other side of the road, stood a huge tent with the legend MERLIN written in bold black letters at regular intervals, the acronym for Medicine Emergency Relief International. The aid agencies, in fierce competition with each other, were not shy of advertising themselves. I counted 29 of them in the space of a single morning as they sped purposefully in their jeeps between the hotel overlooking Lake Kivu and the UNHCR compound further down the road, which also overlooked the lake. Ironically, the UNHCR compound was the most heavily fortified of any I saw in that small town, surrounded as it was by a 10 foot high wall and an equally imposing iron gate, which meant that the view, the reason for its superb location, had been forfeited for a reason that was difficult to fathom. The town was perfectly safe at all times of the day and night. Still, with all those refugees wandering about the place...

I thought of visiting the MERLIN tent but the area around it had been cordoned off and a self-important man in his middle years, happy no doubt for the work, already appeared harassed enough by the untidy group of refugees sitting on the ground in front of the entrance waiting to be seen. So I just stood there and watched. Presently one of the refugees, a bearded man in his thirties, came over and asked me if I wanted to buy some Zairean money. In the confusion of flight he had omitted to change his notes in Zaire, he said, and he couldn't get a decent price for them in Rwanda. This wasn't surprising. The Zairean currency had finally succumbed to Wole Soyinka's prophecy and was now effectively 'shit paper'. The notes themselves came in denominations of 50,000 with the obligatory picture of President Mobutu in his younger days (in the days when he left no 'hen' alone) but who was now recuperating in France following an operation for prostate cancer in Switzerland, the trip itself only made possible because he was smart enough to put his faith in currencies that came in much smaller denominations, and who should know better?

By now it was late afternoon and overcast. It was the tail-end of the rainy season: it had rained heavily the day before the refugees had begun their long march, and it looked set to do so again. I started back for my hotel when I saw the photographer, young and blonde and pretty, hovering a couple of feet above a small black child, two years old perhaps, who was sitting cross-legged in the dirt, dressed only in a ragged T-shirt. After a moment she paused in her labours, smiled half-apologetically at the adults around her in tacit acknowledgement of the brutal arithmetic that she was busy exploiting here, and gently tilted the child's head just a fraction more upwards so that his big black liquid eyes were more obviously directed towards the heavens, and then she resumed her click click clicking, working away diligently while The African Child obligingly held his pose and the adults continued to stare. I wondered how much she had paid them. Most of the refugees were hungry, which is part of the condition of being a refugee. I had seen them scramble without any hint of pride or shame for the biscuits thrown by local people from passing vehicles.

In Kigali the following day, which was my last, I recounted the story of the photographer to a young Rwandan man I had met when I first arrived in the country the previous week. The image had remained very vivid in my mind. This was not only because of its inherent vulgarity and its questionable ethics but, more importantly, because it seemed to symbolise everything that was wrong about the western adventure taking place in that border town, of which more presently. At any rate my friend heard me out in silence and then told me that he had in fact come across the exact same thing on the steps of the main post office just the other day and he and some others had forced the photographer to destroy the film because, he said, he wasn't about to be party to such an image appearing on the pages of the western press, which was where it was headed.

I sympathised with my friend but I couldn't agree with him, not least because his actions made absolutely no difference to the balance of power that gave rise to the affront in the first place. The problem went much deeper, to the very heart of why the continent kept on generating one tragedy after another, but I didn't say anything because he had much better reason than I did to vent his anger. He was a member of the country's Tutsi minority, for which reason he had lost seven members of his immediate family between April and July 1994. This was when the more extremist elements within the majority Hutu population, aided and abetted by a bankrupt Hutu government, unleashed a new round of genocide against their hated enemy. Only his mother and one brother were now left. 'When I remember about it I feel to cry,' he said. Nor was his story unique. Another Tutsi I spoke with, a journalist, counted off the number of nephews and nieces he had lost in the same period: seven out of eight from one sister; six out of seven from another; both the children of a third; the only child of a fourth... All his sisters had also lost their husbands into the bargain. His own wife was still missing.

Here is part of a transcript from a private radio station, the since-defunct Radio-Television Libre des Mille Collines, whose role in a largely illiterate and predominantly peasant society was absolutely central to the attempted genocide:

> Remember that our movement starts from cellules, our movement starts from sectors and communes. The President told you that a tree without leaves and without roots dies... Our cellule leaders get together. Whoever enters your cellule, see him. If he is an *ibyitso* [accomplice] crush him and make sure he does not get out. Do not let him get out alive. I recently told somebody who was showing off, saying he was from the PL [Parti Liberal], and said to him that the mistake we made in 1959, although I was a child, was that we let you get out. I asked him if he has never heard of the history of the Falashas who went back to their land in Israel from Ethiopia and he told me he did not know it. I told him, 'You don't know how to listen and read. I'd like to tell you that your home is in Ethiopia and we will dump you in Nyabaroongo [river] for you to arrive quickly.'

Even moderate Hutus, *ibyitso*, were targeted for extermination by the Hutu militias, the *interahamwe*, 'those who stay together'. It was estimated that up to a million people were killed in the course of this new round of madness, one-eighth of the population. One talks in such large numbers where this tiny, mountainous country is concerned. But why such hatred? Both speak the same language, Kinyarwanda, which is more widely used than French, the other language they share, and both worship the same gods; however: 'I can tell a Hutu just by shaking his hand. I don't have to look at him at all. I just know.' Even the visitor quickly finds the Tutsi arrogance overbearing. The smart young man who told me this in the bar of a hotel, and who was later to cheat me in a small transaction even as he drank my beer, was anxious to make me understand that the Hutus were primitive, backward, and intellectually inferior; that they had low foreheads and fat cheeks and sturdy limbs in order that they might work long hours in the fields, which was where they belonged, where they were happiest until they started getting notions about making it in the city; and that the Hutu problem was compounded by their tendency to breed early, as young as 16 for many of the females, which was how come there were so many of them, 85 per cent of the population at the last count and climbing. In short, he said, by now thoroughly excited and only just managing to keep his voice down, the Hutus were only one step up from the gorillas in the jungle mist that the *muzungus*, the white people, were so interested in studying and preserving.

THE genocide in Rwanda only ceased when a rebel Tutsi force invaded the country from neighbouring Uganda and toppled the government, whereupon an estimated one million Hutus (those numbers again), among them members of the *interahamwe* too frightened or too incompetent to fight a properly trained army, fled into exile in eastern Zaire. And now trouble had started again when that country's own home-grown Tutsis, with or without assistance from the new government in Rwanda, took advantage of President Mobutu's absence to launch a civil war against one of the continent's longest-running and most corrupt dictatorships. Not that Mobutu's presence in the country could have done much to prevent their initial success. According to the rebel leader, Laurent Kabila, the Zairean soldiers 'flee when the fighting starts' on account of the fact that they've had no training and no pay for the last six years, the point being that a demoralised army, which had long been encouraged to terrorise the populace for their daily bread, was hardly in a position to stage a coup. This was one reason why Mobutu was able to survive as the Number One Citizen for more than 30 years. The soldiers couldn't even protect the genuine refugees, who were used as hostages by the *interahamwe* until they were set free by the Zairean rebels — with or without the help of the Rwandan forces stationed just the other side of the border.

So here were the refugees, two years later, retracing their footsteps to their towns and villages and farms, some of them as far as Kigali 150 kilometres away. And here we all were, too, the western media with our flak jackets and our stout walking boots and our yellow accreditation cards issued by the Ministry of Information at US$50 a time (the Rwandan government was making money out of the unfolding tragedy) watching them return, except that there was nobody from the African media to report what one might have assumed — naively, it turned out — to be first and foremost an African story. There were Italians and Belgians and Swiss and Dutch and Swedish and Japanese and Canadian and French; there was George Alagiah from the BBC and Christiane Amanpour from CNN; there were two Paris-based Lebanese journalists working for

Kuwaiti TV; there was even someone from the *Philadelphia Enquirer* and another from the *Baltimore Sun*.

But nobody from Africa. There was nobody from Kenya, the regional power with good reason to be nervous about ambitious young men in the bush plotting to overthrow the old guard. There was nobody from South Africa, the continent's economic and military muscle, which lacks a coherent foreign policy more than two years after majority rule. There was nobody from oil-rich Nigeria, where US$12 billion of government revenue can disappear in a period of six months, enough, surely, to feed and clothe and transport every single one of those refugees walking across the border. There wasn't even anybody from the Pan-African News Agency, the information arm of the Organisation of African Unity (OAU), whose 'Conflict Management Division' was just then holding a series of meetings in far away Addis Ababa in order to hammer out a continental position on events in the Great Lakes region. According to a report by the Voice of America, which was also covering the OAU deliberations on behalf of Kenya and South Africa and Nigeria, the OAU initiative was itself 'sponsored largely by the West'. This made sense of sorts since the information that the OAU was basing its deliberations on was also courtesy of the otherwise reviled western media. Of course, the western media necessarily had its own agenda, for instance making sure we understood that the OAU had become so enfeebled that it could no longer underwrite meetings in its own continent, or omitting to tell us that certain pictures of suffering Africans were deliberately stage-managed in the interests of careers.

What we were watching, in effect, was a phenomenon in which the West was talking to the West in order to raise yet more money in the West, which also meant that the African refugees in whose name all this activity was taking place were curiously peripheral; were, in fact, rendered invisible despite (or even because of) their huge numbers. It was for this reason, after all, that the photographer could so easily overcome the qualms she felt about what she was doing with that small child. It was for this reason, also, that a young woman aid worker responsible for 'logistics' (she had a walkie-talkie to prove it) could say so casually, 'There were five deaths yesterday. It isn't a large number. Three of them were under five.'

The aid worker in question, four years out of an English university, was giving the low-down to two young Englishmen, both journalists, new on the scene and raring to go. She didn't mean to sound offhand or callous about the corpses currently at the mercy of her sexual vanity, but who could blame her when she was being told at every turn that it was apparently impossible to find a single Rwandan capable of doing her job? Or that Africans, when they were employed by the (presumably) more 'enlightened' agencies, were worth less than their western counterparts? One such agency, for instance, paid an American doctor US$4,000 per month and his Kenyan colleague US$1,900, and yet there was absolutely no difference between them in age or qualifications. Ditto the nurses: US$2,500 and US$1,000 respectively. Naturally, the African staff were disgruntled by this blatant demonstration of racism, which was how come they complained to me; on the other hand, dollars is dollars. Besides, where were the African agencies and/or governments in all of this, content as they were to let foreigners feed their brothers and sisters? Poverty wasn't the issue but political will, or the lack of it, but then poverty was never the issue, only the excuse.

And then there was the awkward, ever-present fact of the refugees themselves, the hundreds of thousands of men and women and children endlessly walking. The refugees hadn't been created by the West; they had been created by Africa itself. Worse yet, a good number of them in whose name the BBC and CNN and the *Philadelphia Enquirer* and the *Baltimore Sun* and the 29 aid agencies had booked every available room in the small border town were themselves murderers and collaborators, but were now relying — as ever! — on the conscience of western taxpayers to spirit them back to their homes in one piece against the day when they feel moved to start another round of slaughter.

The human migration we witnessed was unquestionably biblical in terms of the numbers involved; on the other hand, one could hardly say that they were seeking the promised land since they had already been in possession of it but had decided that they would rather forfeit it than live next door to a fellow Rwandan who was shorter or taller or had a slightly flatter nose... This was the reality, and not made any more palatable by the fact that the continent itself (and not only Rwanda) appeared to believe that the solution to all problems African lay in the hands of fresh young graduates from the West, people for whom Africa could never be more than a career opportunity. ❑

JULIAN PETLEY

The year of the bully

British TV censorship is largely a thing of the past. Far more threatening is the concert of pusillanimous management, government intimidation and the machinations of spin doctors

TELEVISION censorship in Britain is pretty rare these days. That is, if you define censorship narrowly as the permanent banning of an entire programme which is pulled from the schedules after its transmission has been publicly announced. By this definition, only two programmes were censored in 1996: the *Without Walls* 'Psychoanalysing Diana', which Channel 4 pulled in May after it had been criticised by several newspapers and health professionals, and the satirical comedy *Brass Eye* in November.

However, if we widen the definition to include any concerted activities that threaten to narrow the range of views and perspectives available on television, then there has certainly been a great deal to worry about. Three trends in particular seem to be intensifying: bullying and intimidation by government and the client press (most notably the *Mail* and its grotesque, self-caricatural hate campaign against Channel 4); attempts at news management by an ever-growing army of lawyers, public relations people and spin doctors; and, in the face of the above, an increasing pusillanimity, feebleness and willingness to engage in self-censorship on the part of the broadcasting organisations.

As Martin Gregory put it in July 1995 after picking up £55,000 in libel damages and costs from the government as the price for the Department of Trade and Industry's squalid campaign of vilification against his *Dispatches* TV programme 'The Torture Trail', 'Truth has become an endangered species in the reporting of British corporate and political life. The Thatcher/Tebbit blitz on television journalism in the mid-1980s has left the landscape irrevocably changed. Politicians and companies now employ PR henchmen, spin doctors and lawyers to bully the journalists and media outlets they cannot compromise.'

A similar point was made more recently by environmental campaigner George Monbiot when he noted that 'as potential plaintiffs become more enterprising, pursuing editors with threatening letters and injunctions long before their material sees the light of day, media lawyers are becoming more and more cautious and journalists ever less robust in their attempts to bring large corporations or powerful individuals to account.'

Indeed, television's handling of environmental issues provides a case in point. Environmental protest is rapidly becoming criminalised, protesters are being routinely and systematically roughed up and subjected to the full 'surveillance state' treatment, but where are the televisual equivalents of, for example, *Guardian* environment correspondent John Vidal's award-winning reports from the Newbury bypass site? One of these — about attempts by the Central Office of Information, the under-sheriff of Newbury, the police and the Highway's Agency to prevent Vidal from witnessing what was happening to the protesters — provides us, implicitly, with the answer: 'managed' out of existence by an unholy combination of official heavy-handedness and timorous televisual complicity. In broadcasting terms, environmental protest — one of the key political issues of our times — has become as sensitive a topic as nuclear arms and left-wing politics used to be in the days of the Cold War: a black hole which programme-makers enter at their peril. The only sustained visual account of what is now going on in this area is provided by *samizdat* video newsreels such as 'Undercurrents' — a fitting comment on the increasingly authoritarian state in which we now live.

The Conservative government is, of course, a past master at the art of bullying broadcasters — remember *Death on the Rock* and *Secret Society* for example? Over the past year or so, the Tories have revived the so-called Media Monitoring Unit, Conservative Party chairman Dr Brian Mawhinney has attacked Radio 4's *Today* programme, the *House of Cards* trilogy, *The Politician's Wife* and *Week-Ending* as anti-Tory; and he and health minister Stephen Dorrell jointly attacked an episode of *Casualty* for allegedly maligning the GP fund-holding system. Such softening-up of the broadcasters is, of course, one of the most obvious symptoms of an approaching general election and, as such, only to be expected.

Considerably more alarming, however, was BBC director-general John Birt's response to Mawhinney's all-too-predictable bullying over the allegedly 'hostile' tone of an Anna Ford interview with Kenneth Clarke, especially when compared with James Naughtie's with Tony Blair on the

M11 motorway protest, London 1994: 'Undercurrents' in action

same edition of *Today* (an achingly over-familiar Tory whipping-boy). In a letter leaked to the media, Birt wrote to Mawhinney that, in the case of the Clarke interview 'there were more interruptions than were appropriate', adding that 'more thought should have been given to ensuring greater consistency of approach to two major political interviews in the same edition.' Displaying a commendable, if atypical, sense of understatement, a Tory Central Office spokeswoman stated that the letter showed 'significant concessions by the director-general'. However, for once the Tory press got something right — they called it an apology.

This, however, was as nothing compared to the revelation in September that the BBC had axed two *Newsnight* investigations by Martin Gregory into British Airways. One of the programmes had examined anti-competitive 'dirty tricks' against Virgin and other rivals, and the other looked at the quite extraordinary campaign of harassment and intimidation of John Gorman, a former policeman who had the temerity to complain about a piece of glass which he found in his drink whilst on a BA flight to New York. Gregory had in fact already made a *Newsnight* report on the Gorman affair, and this was broadcast in August 1994. A leaked memo in the wake of the programme from John Birt to Tony Hall, the head of BBC News, gave hints of the problems to come. Birt complained of 'too much innuendo' and 'too little evidence' of a link between the Gorman persecution and 'named individuals at the top of the organisation', including the BA chief executive Robert Ayling. The programme made him 'uneasy', it showed 'no sophisticated understanding of how institutions work' and 'the events described were incredible.' Indeed they are, but not in the sense that Birt implies.

When BA realised that at least one follow-up programme was in the offing they began a PR onslaught against the BBC. In this they were advised by Lowe Bell, who were engaged by BA in 1993 specifically to counter the swelling flood of 'dirty tricks' stories. But, up until April 1996, Lowe Bell was also acting for the BBC in the run-up to the Charter renewal. And Sir Tim Bell himself had advised Birt some three years earlier in the very public furore over his tax arrangements. In April 1995, Robert Ayling wrote to Tony Hall expressing concern over the choice of Gregory to make the follow-up, as he considered the original programme 'neither fair nor accurate'. Hall's position can't have been made any easier by the fact that Ayling was a personal friend of his boss, John Birt.

In spite of a massive campaign of obstruction by BA, one programme

IN THE NEWS: UK

was completed and was ready for transmission in November 1995. It had been shown to the BBC's lawyers and, after substantial cuts, pronounced a fair risk. The BBC then took further advice from a big libel practice, and decided not to broadcast the programme. Production on the second one was halted shortly thereafter.

Now whilst it is entirely understandable that BA and its PR company should have done everything possible to damage and, ultimately, destroy a programme that lifts the lid on a most unsavoury can of worms, it is hard to disagree with Gregory's judgement that the BBC's cave-in in the face of BA's PR barrage is 'a disgrace which betrays everything that BBC director-general John Birt claims that BBC journalism stands for'. As always in these cases, it was not programme-makers who were to blame but their betrayal by senior managers and the craven culture which they have created within the BBC. As Gregory himself has noted, Bell knew enough about the BBC to understand that the weakest part of the BBC's journalistic set-up was its senior management, and when his PR men went to work they directed their best efforts at these 'gullible victims for their black arts'.

In the meantime, Gregory's book on BA, which actually goes beyond the material contained in the aborted *Newsnight* programmes, has been published by Warners (hardly a monument to illegality and subversion) without the slightest comeback from bullying BA.

And if this sorry tale reminds you of something it could just be this. As reported in *Index* 2/1995, in April 1994 Central Television halted production of a potentially explosive *Cook Report* which blew the gaff on the lobbying activities of a certain Ian Greer. Central has always maintained that the programme was dropped because the story 'did not come up to scratch' and 'did not make a *Cook Report*', but cynics have persisted in drawing attention to the close links between Greer and the upper echelons of Central and Carlton which merged in early 1994. Thus it was left to the *Guardian* to scoop the Greer story. Indeed, one of the many disappointments of the collapse of the Greer/Hamilton case is that, had the libel action gone ahead, Central would have been forced by the *Guardian* to show the *Cook* material in court. Now we may never know. ❏

Julian Petley *is head of communication and information studies at Brunel University, UK. He is co-editor of* Ill Effects: The Media Violence Debate *(Routledge, 1997, £12.99pb, £40 hb)*

Hong Kong goes back

For the first time in the history of modern empire, a colony is relinquished not to freedom, but back into the embrace of an older and more ruthless emperor. It's still six months to the handover, but Beijing has put its man in position and Britain has turned its back ingloriously after a century and a half. A dab of democracy too little and too late; out-dated security laws still on the statute book; refugees and dissidents from the mainland who sought sanctuary in the territory abandoned to their fate. Optimists point to Hong Kong's economy or the close ties of family, history and culture as safeguards from Beijing's worst excesses and note the changes already wrought by the one on the other. But Hong Kong's proponents of free expression, democracy and civil rights fear the worst

File compiled by Judith Vidal-Hall with Yang Lian
With contributions from Article 19 and
Reporters Sans Frontières

Left: Tiananmen Square, Beijing: countdown clock; Credit: Ron Giling/Panos

CHINA		HONG KONG
First dynasty (Shang)	16th–11th BC	
Emperor Qin takes HK	214 BC	HK to China
Opium War	1839–41	
	1842	Treaty of Nanjing UK takes HK (population 5,000)
Taiping Rebellion	1850–64	
	1860	Beijing Convention cedes Kowloon to UK
Reform Movement	1895–98	
	1898	New Territories, marine islands, Kowloon & HK leased to UK for 99 years
Boxer Rebellion	1900	
Nationalist Revolution	1911–12	
Warlord Period	1917–27	
Birth of Communist Party	1921	
Birth of Red Army	1927	
Nationalist Rule	1927–49	
Long March	1934–36	
War with Japan/Yanan Period	1937–45	
	1941–45	Japanese occupation
Civil War	1946–49	
National Day	1 Oct 1949	HK population swells with mainland exiles (from 1.5 million to 1.8 million 1941-1949)
Korean War	1950–53	
Great Leap Forward	1958–60	
	1962	Estimated 100,000 Chinese flee to HK in one month
Sino–Soviet Split	1963	
Cultural Revolution	1966–76	
First dissident manifesto	1973	
Tiananmen Incident	5 April 1976	
Death of Mao Zedong	9 Sept 1976	
Deng takes power	1978	
Democracy Wall Movement	1979–80	
Founding of Shenzhen SEZ	1980	
Rural Reforms	1978–85	
Industrial Reforms	1984	Joint Sino–British Declaration providing for return of HK to Chinese rule, 1 July 1997
Democracy Movement	Jan–June 1989	
Beijing Massacre	June 1989	Millions protest against Beijing Massacre
	1990	China passes the Basic Law for the governance of HK after the 1997 takeover
Deng visits SEZs	1992	Chris Patten becomes last British governor of HK & introduces electoral reform
Start of Deng's decline	1994	
Crackdown on dissidents	1994–96	First democratic elections held for HK's administrative body, Legco. 16 out of 20 seats are taken by the Democrats.
	1996	China vows to disband Legco after the takeover China forms the Preparatory Committee to choose a provisional leglislature & chief executive to take over from Legco after the takeover.
HK due to go back to China	1 July 1997	
Portuguese colony of Macao due to return to China	1999	

JOHN GITTINGS

Cost of a miracle

Deng Xiaoping's reforms have changed the face of China: the economy has made epic strides, cities fly the banners of western capitalism, a new middle class aspires to full membership of the consumer society. In the process, political reform got left behind, repression of dissidents is as harsh as ever and a growing gap between rich and poor, town and country, threaten the stability of the Middle Kingdom

THE LONG MARCH of Chinese society has been under way since Mao Zedong died 20 years ago. It had already started, beneath the surface of the 'Cultural Revolution' (1966-76), while he was still alive. It is as stupendous an epic as the original Long March in the mid-1930s when Mao led the Communists across China to a new revolutionary base. To adapt Marx, it is a journey from the realm of necessity to the realm of freedom, but it still has a very long way to go.

The world outside China has paid only intermittent attention to this difficult and painful process which involves 1.1 billion people on a scale almost too huge to comprehend. Only the moments of drama attract headlines: those in China who struggle for reform and democracy do so mostly in silence, with far less encouragement than was given in the past to those making a similar effort in the Soviet Union and Eastern Europe. By joining the world market, Deng Xiaoping has earned a large measure of international immunity.

On 30 June this year the 'return to the motherland' of another six and a half millions, in Hong Kong, should focus our attention more acutely. They are about to become part of the story which till now they have witnessed at close hand but apart. They do so from a unique position, already enjoying most of the freedoms which are much harder to secure across the border. They have the advantage that these benefits are still guaranteed to them under international treaty — but only if the outside world (and particularly Britain) chooses to monitor what happens to them and protest if it is needed.

China has made vast progress in the last two decades. In economic policy, the results have already been breathtaking. When weeping crowds filled Tiananmen Square two decades ago, no-one could have imagined that China would jettison within a few years the whole model of alternative development — from people's communes to national self-reliance — which underpinned Mao's 'socialist road'. China has joined the global market and offers an entirely different model of participation in the 'international division of labour'.

Yet the transformation of China's economic base has not been matched in the superstructure of Chinese politics. Those cracks which did emerge have been arrested — often in a literal sense. The first fissure was seen even before Mao's death, in April 1976, when thousands of Beijing residents gathered on Tiananmen Square in a huge wave of grief for the earlier death of Premier Zhou Enlai: a pretext to demonstrate against the ultra-left clique (the Gang of Four led by Mao's wife Jiang Qing) which had usurped power.

Their poems and manifestos, written in chalk — or blood — on the pavement, were washed out of sight by Beijing's entire fleet of water carts. A furious Communist Party leadership forced half of Beijing to parade through the streets with limp flags in denunciation. Three years later, in the street newspapers and posters of Beijing's Democracy Wall (1979-80) — briefly approved by the new leadership of Deng Xiaoping — this new movement for social justice and democracy, at first still socialist democracy, seemed to gather strength. Yet the decade and a half since then has seen an increasingly unequal struggle between the voices of reform and the instruments of repression.

This winter Wei Jingsheng, China's most-imprisoned dissident, settles to the second year of his second jail term of 14 years, in a prison camp on a north Chinese salt marsh, sharing an unheated cell with other hostile inmates. As a young Red Guard 30 years ago, Wei had been shaken by the poverty and oppression that he witnessed while roaming China to 'make revolution'. Once he saw a young woman begging for food by the railway track: she had no clothes so had daubed her body with mud and ashes. Such sights were the start of real 're-education' for many young Chinese. Wei's uncompromising call for democracy — on Democracy Wall — led to his first long prison sentence in 1979.

Another veteran dissident, Wang Xizhe — who fled to the US in October 1996 — has been active for even longer. Sent down to the countryside by Chairman Mao, Wang and other idealistic youth worked all day for one or two 'workpoints' — just enough to buy a tube of toothpaste. Seeing rural poverty at first hand, they became sceptical of the official doctrine that 'China's future lies with the peasants'. Wang co-authored the first dissident manifesto 'On socialist democracy and legality' in 1973. It argued that the Communist Party had been hijacked by a 'privileged stratum' which maintained the old Chinese tradition of feudal autocracy under a different name.

Many feudal habits have been discarded, but a regime which decrees that political dissent should be treated as a counter-revolutionary threat is still profoundly autocratic. This mismatch between the pace of economic and political reform in post-Mao China remains a fundamental though largely hidden flaw in Chinese society. Any attempt to reach a conclusion on this period, or to predict where China is heading, must acknowledge both the magnitude of what has been achieved in changing the face of China, and the extent to which many deeper features remain largely unaltered.

The Gang of Four was arrested within a month of Mao's death: everyone agreed that their 'ultra-left excesses' would have to be purged from the system. But when I visited China again in 1978, only one far-sighted Chinese scholar predicted that the Cultural Revolution — not just the Gang — would be repudiated. Many people were shocked to learn about the emergence of a system of elite schools for clever children, and to discover that bonuses were being offered to factory managers and workers.

China had struggled to survive for 25 years against a subtle combination of US and Soviet hostility — hence the strategic need for 'self-reliance'. Though Richard Nixon opened the door in 1972, while Mao was still alive, China was still remote and the outside world was unknown. In the whole of the capital city, there was only one set of automatic doors — at the entrance to the Beijing Hotel. Large crowds gathered on the pavement to see them in operation. In 1978, foreign beverages — alcoholic and soft drinks — were served for the first time in this and other hotels (which were barred to Chinese). For a few glorious months, whisky was on sale in full glasses for the same price as Coca Cola. Beijing shut down early: it was impossible to buy a meal after seven in the evening.

Beijing today is unrecognisable to anyone who remembers the 1970s. There is a surplus of five-star hotels, three separate ring-roads, scores of high-rise office blocks, dozens of department stores selling more foreign than Chinese goods, hundreds of restaurants open till late with strings of fairy lights outside — and endless traffic jams. Out of sight in the suburbs, there are encampments of migrant workers on whose cheap labour the building boom depends.

Progress across China is more uneven, but even in the deep interior, every medium-sized town will have a pocket of Hong Kong-style shops and housing. Small towns, even villages, have their own karaoke bars. And from Beijing to the countryside, the lone traveller will receive advice which would have once been unthinkable: 'Don't go out alone late at night.' 'Watch out for highwaymen on the long-distance buses!'

Modernisation has occurred in three great overlapping waves with the impetus coming both from within and from outside China. First, in the early 1980s, Deng Xiaoping's reforms liberated a huge pent-up torrent of human and material resources. In the countryside, production soared as peasants were given responsibility for farming the land household by household instead of in groups or teams. But they also benefited from the vast capital investment (irrigation works, land enrichment and so on) which had been made during the collective years. In 1983 I visited former communes in central Anhui province whose population had scattered during the Great Leap Forward (1958-60) to beg for food. Each family proudly displayed their 'household contract' book with the state. They were buying their first bicycles and sewing machines. Rural markets, foolishly restricted in the Maoist years, quickly regained their traditional place as centres of craft and commerce.

The New Way of Deng Xiaoping still stressed the goal of socialism but Deng stressed that 'poverty is not socialism'. The battle with capitalism continued, he said, but its outcome would depend on which system could satisfy the needs of more people. At this stage, many Chinese still hoped to return to the collective path once higher living standards had been achieved. They shared the official verdict on the past: Mao had tried to build socialism too fast and had committed too many 'mistakes'.

The second great wave of modernisation came from outside, with Deng's encouragement, and gathered pace in the second half of the 1980s. Deng insisted, against the objections of conservative critics, that 'the world today is an open world' and that China's 'closed-door policy' had led to a state of 'backwardness'. This was essentially correct. He also argued (like the modernisers in the late years of Imperial China) that western techniques could be imported without undermining Chinese values. This proved to be a much more dubious argument.

The new Special Economic Zones on the coast became magnets for development, attracting ambitious young Chinese from all over the mainland. Crucially, they also attracted investment from the wealthy and widespread overseas Chinese community. Foreign cultural and consumption models were copied throughout China. Nine out of 10 popular magazines portrayed foreign fashion, films, sport, food and technology. In the early 1980s, young urban Chinese saved to buy a three-piece suite of furniture. By the end of the decade, they were aiming for a video player.

This opening up coincided with, and sought to take advantage of, the emerging global economy and the revolution in global communications. Hong Kong and other foreign manufacturers transferred production to China to exploit the cheap labour. The zones also fostered criminality, prostitution and large-scale fraud involving senior Chinese officials. In the biggest scam, cadres on Hainan Island, led by the governor himself, imported more than 80,000 cars in less than a year for illegal resale to the mainland.

The giant modernisation of the economy and society was not paralleled in political life. After briefly encouraging the protesters on Beijing's Democracy Wall (1979-80), Deng Xiaoping clamped down, personally approving long jail sentences on Wei Jingsheng and other ex-Red Guard dissidents. Reform-minded intellectuals and progressive Party cadres sought in the mid-1980s to push forward the boundaries of political debate. They called for separation of power between Party and state, for democratic debate and even a free press. In 1989 their efforts combined with a new outburst of protest by students and an emerging workers' movement against Party despotism and corruption. This triple combination — intellectuals, students and workers (backed by millions of ordinary citizens) — terrified the elders of the old guard. The result was the Beijing Massacre on 3-4 June.

A few days before the massacre, I studied a poem pasted on a lamppost in Tiananmen Square. 'Deng Xiaoping suffered criticism (in the Cultural Revolution)', it began, 'and the people raised him up. Now the country does not want him, and the people do not want him. The officials eat the food, the common people labour all year. A small handful get fat, a billion are poor.' This was the authentic voice of millenarian protest in China, heard in the peasant revolts of the imperial past. By now the initial gains of economic reform had become obscured — especially in the countryside — by inflation, corruption and the uneven pace of development between rich and poor areas.

Having suppressed political protest, Deng knew that he had to offer another 'way out' for the majority of Chinese people. The third and current great wave of change was launched by him in 1992 after two years of stagnation. Making his famous 'southern expedition' to the Special Economic Zones adjacent to Hong Kong, he proclaimed a new drive to 'catch up' with the other expanding economies of east Asia. Most of China was now allowed to seek foreign investment and set up its development zones. The state in Beijing still retained control over the levers of macro-economic power, but far more autonomy was granted to the provinces and the market was permitted to overtake the planned sector. Socialism merely meant that the Party remained in charge. The road to prosperity no longer lay through collective struggle: it was to be achieved by individual enterprise. Local newspapers published eulogies not to labour heroes but to model entrepreneurs.

Deng's Great Leap of the 1990s has changed the face of China irrevocably. Western business and media hailed it uncritically as an 'economic miracle': the butcher of Beijing became *Time* magazine's Man of the Year. It has produced enough new wealth — or expectations of wealth — to bury the political protest of the 1980s. (More long jail sentences, including the vicious re-sentencing of Wei Jingsheng, and, most recently in October 1996, student leader Wang Dan, have also deterred dissent.) But if it is a miracle, it is a flawed one. Travelling widely in provincial China over the past five years, I have seen many of its limitations.

In many areas the gains of agriculture have slowed down or been reversed, while local Party cadres increase their extortion, levying illegal taxes and fines. Millions of peasants flock to the cities creating the sort of underclass long found in other Third World countries. Rural health and education have suffered as the collective structures which support them have been weakened. The current policy is also familiar elsewhere: urban wealth is accumulated on the basis of peasant blood and sweat, and on the theory that some of the proceeds will trickle down to the rural areas.

Urban growth has been phenomenal but wasteful of resources. New 'development zones' are often idle, taking up valuable arable land. The intense struggle for profitable business opportunities encourages more corruption. The successful aspire to a Hong Kong lifestyle which is openly displayed with elite housing precincts, luxury automobiles, exclusive golf and business clubs. Benefits are not confined to the few: a sizeable new middle class has emerged forming the basis of an incipient civil society which China has never known before. But there is also a new urban underclass of the unemployed, the very poor and the rapidly expanding criminal world.

The biggest casualty of the 'economic miracle' has been the environment, already under severe pressure for many decades as population expanded. The pollution of air and water, the lack of safety at work, the despoiling of the countryside, the illegal mining for gold (which has killed hundreds of prospectors), is reminiscent of the early industrial revolution in the West. These problems are compounded by a late twentieth-century phenomenon: China now plans to become a 'great car economy', producing millions of new private automobiles in the next decade.

In 20 years China has shifted from one extreme to the other in its development strategy: a middle way was briefly contemplated but soon swept aside. Now the big question — which some in Beijing are beginning to understand — is whether China can learn from the failures as well as the successes of the western capitalist system. China's political culture has changed much less. Young Chinese are either extremely cynical about their own society or intensely patriotic — sometimes the two together. Politics, they say, is less interesting than making money. The mood is sustained by the outside world's continued eagerness to invest in China and employ its cheap labour: China's wealthy diaspora of overseas Chinese confers a special advantage. But the mismatch between political and economic change remains: a crisis in the Party after Deng's death, or an economic downturn (or a combination of both) could revive popular demands for a more just and democratic society. Then the crowds might even return to Tiananmen Square. ❏

John Gittings is foreign leader-writer at the Guardian, and first visited China in 1971. His latest book Real China: From Cannibalism to Karaoke was published in 1996 by Simon & Schuster (London). It will be published in paperback (£7.99) in February

Tiananmen Square, 5 April 1976: in the first great protest while Mao Zedong is still alive, a brave young man reads out a manifesto against the Gang of Four

China since Mao

Tiananmen Square, 8 April 1976: unwilling Beijing citizens are marshalled with flags for an official demonstration against the recent genuine protest

Shengli Oilfield, Shangdong, October 1978: a roadside poster shows Chinese youth speeding ahead to modernise the country by the Year 2000

Democracy Wall, November 1978: against a bus garage in the western district of Beijing, dissenting wall posters are pasted up — and copied by eager activists

Tiananmen Square, 5 April 1980: the portrait of a loyal Communist, Zhang Zhixin, killed in the Cultural Revolution, is placed against the Martyrs' Memorial by sympathisers

Sports Stadium, Beijing, 1980: new advertisements for sports goods begin to elbow out Mao portraits and 'Long Lie' slogans in the capital

Shanghai, 1982: film advertisement for 1930s novel Midnight, *banned in the Cultural Revolution, by Mao Dun*

Shanghai, 1984: ex-Red Guards, marooned in the countryside after being 'sent down' in the Cultural Revolution, protest at their exile with cartoons showing their hard life

旗帜鲜明地自制动乱

89.5.21
仁明作

Beijing University, May 1989: satirical cartoon attacks Premier Li Peng after he declared martial law. 'He keeps the flag clean by stirring up turmoil.'

Tiananmen Square, May 1989: the Martyrs' Memorial is festooned with pro-democracy banners and posters

Anyang, north China, 1991: new commercial centre in an ancient city: the stalls stock lurid sex and crime magazines — but no politics allowed

Wuxuan, southwest China, 1993: students study exam results for college entrance: their one chance to leave this isolated country town

Zhengzhou, north China, 1993: job-seeking peasant migrants wait for train outside railway station

All photos except 1, 8, 9 by John Gittings

Who should you believe?

N o one seems to know who or what to trust about what's happening in the world these days. Is nuclear terrorism running rampant? How close is Iraq to building a bomb? Are India and Pakistan on the brink of war?

Find out when you subscribe to *The Bulletin of the Atomic Scientists*. We'll bring you voices from around the world reporting on everything from plutonium to peace talks. You don't have to be a rocket scientist to get it—just subscribe.

HARRY WU

Inside the *laogai*

No totalitarian rule can exist without a machinery of suppression to maintain its order. In addition to an elaborate judicial and administrative system, it needs a political theory to justify the operations of such a system. Nazi Germany, based on its *Herrenvolk* theory and National Socialism, established its immense concentration camp system. Likewise, Lenin and Stalin, on the theory of exterminating the exploiter classes and establishing the Communist revolution, organised a gulag system.

The Chinese Communist Party's labour-reform camp system is no different from that of the Communist power in the former Soviet Union, in its political theory, brutality, violation of principles of humanism or the scale of its forced labour. Nevertheless, it does eclipse the Soviet gulag in the following two areas.

Firstly, production and economic results are highly stressed. Forced labour in the *laogai* camps plays an important role in China's national economy. It places great emphasis on effectiveness, profits and economic results that are standard norms in average enterprises. To strive for greater profits, the *laogai* camp system does all in its power to escalate from a punitive form of labour to that seen in modern enterprises.

Secondly, greater emphasis is placed on destroying the *laogai* inmates mentally and ideologically. The *laogai* camp system possesses a set of measures and methods of brainwashing, ie 'thought reform'. For the Chinese Communists, the aim is not to destroy a hostile element physically through violence, but to destroy him mentally and ideologically, while threatening him with violence. Thus, the 'reformed' prisoners, deprived of freedom and dignity, but grateful for being allowed to exist, contribute their sweat and blood to their rulers, while those who 'reformed' them are crowned with laurels of 'socialist revolutionary humanism'.

Some *laogai* survivors have written accounts of their experiences, but

Liu Shanqing (second from right) and colleagues in the Hong Kong Patriotic Alliance for a Democratic China stage a demonstration in support of political prisoner Chen Ximing in summer 1995

only a few. There are memoirs, like Jean Pasqualini's *Prisoner of Mao*, Nien Cheng's *Life and Death in Shanghai* and my own *Bitter Winds*. A few are academic research works on *laogai* camps, such as Jean-Luc Domenach's *China's Archipelago* and my *Laogai: The Chinese Gulag*.

Memoirs of survivors portray only a small part of the thousands upon thousands of indescribable nightmares that have occurred in the People's Republic of China. They are so difficult to comprehend not only for western journalists and readers, but for Chinese readers and writers as well, unless they experienced them body and soul. As the Chinese proverb says: 'All bamboo on South Hill made into writing brushes, the crimes are too numerous to record; all squalls in East Sea drained, the evils are too rooted to eradicate.' ❏

Harry Wu spent 19 years inside China's prison and labour camps. He was released in 1979 and went into exile in the USA. He returned to China secretly three times to document the use of slave labour in prison camps. His latest book, Troublemaker, *was published in 1996 by Chatto and Windus*

© *From the foreword to* Eighteen Layers of Hell: Stories from the Chinese Gulag *by Kate Saunders (Cassell, 1996)*

SUSAN WHITFIELD

Only one death

The lessons of a long history of dissent are not lost on today's workers, peasants and intellectuals

Portrait of Qu Yuan (1498)

AFTER one of their number was punished by the state for 'incorrect political criticism', Chinese students of the most prestigious university gathered in front of the government buildings. They presented a petition protesting against the sentence handed down to the university vice-rector, who had supported their classmate. Their main grievance was against corrupt government. Established officials who had dismissed their generation as 'wild and reckless', incapable of thinking of anything but their own pleasure, were forced to revise their opinions. One sent them a letter of support — at some personal risk. Nevertheless, the vice-rector's punishment was carried out and corruption continued to flourish. It will be many years before the government falls, but this was one indicator of its decline.

This is not a description of present events in China: they happened in 798. The vice-rector was an official named Yuan Cheng. He had been persuaded into government service because of his reputation as an honest and principled man — qualities felt by many to be lacking in most officials close to the emperor. It was over a decade, however, before he justified this reputation, memorialising the emperor in protest at the banishment of one of the chief ministers. Demotion to the post of the vice-rector of the Imperial University was his punishment. Three years later he was in trouble again when a university student, about to be exiled, was found in his house. Yuan Cheng was also exiled, but by his virtuous deeds he had shown himself to be a Confucian gentleman and history would judge him kindly. After all, as a ninth-century writer pointed out:

> A chief minister may control a man's destiny for a decade or so, but the historian will cause his name to flourish for hundreds of thousands of years or to simply fade away.

Most literati-officials — although some were themselves employed by the state history office — did not leave this responsibility solely to the historians. They wrote their own record of events to propagate their version of history. The junior official, Liu Zongyuan in his letter of support to the students, expresses this aim:

> You are now directing all your energies to just purposes... The words of you students are not solely for yourselves, but are relevant for the entire state. ...I have set brush to paper because I want to encourage your noble intentions, and to give future historians material for their historical narratives.

Liu Zongyuan may well have had previous student demonstrations in mind when he wrote this — several are recorded. The educated knew their history and used it 'to illuminate the present'. The students demonstrating in Tiananmen Square in 1976, 1986 and 1989, compared their protests with an event from more recent history: the 4 May demonstrations of 1919. But they too were well aware of an older model of dissent: that of Qu Yuan, the paragon of the honest official who was punished for daring to criticise.

Qu Yuan served at the court of Chu — a kingdom bordering the Yellow River — in the third century BC. His advice was ignored — to the detriment of the state — and his enemies gained control. He subsequently drowned himself, although not before writing a considerable body of poetry venting his feelings. He is China's first named poet and by means of his pen he enabled history, rather than his peers, to judge his actions. And they found favourably, probably not least because of the excellence of his verse. The dragon-boat festival, still celebrated today, is a commemoration of his death. The importance of literature for immortality was thereafter well-recognised. The following passage is from China's first historian, Sima Qian, explaining why he accepted the humiliating punishment of castration instead of resorting to the more honourable alternative of suicide. It was written in the second century BC.

A man has only one death. Though I might be weak and cowardly and seek shamefully to prolong my life, yet I know full well the difference between what ought to be followed and what rejected. The reason I have refused to die is that I grieve that I have things in my heart that I have not been able to express fully, and I am shamed to think that after I am gone my writings will not be known to posterity.

The men of antiquity who were rich and noble yet whose names have vanished away are numerous. It is only those who were masterful and sure, the truly extraordinary men, who are remembered... they wrote of past affairs in order to hand down their thoughts to future generations.

In contrast, several hundred Confucian officials who, according to some historical sources, were buried alive in the period between the lives of Qu Yuan and Sima Qian,

China 2nd century BC: scholars are buried alive

remain anonymous. The First Emperor — he of the terracotta army — is held responsible for this act. He was also alert to the subversive power of the written word: he ordered the burning of all books of history, philosophy and literature — except for the records of his own state.

The officials met their earthy end because, as the antagonistic chief minister said: 'they study the past in order to criticise the present.' This was true. Officials could hardly say to the emperor's face that he was wrong (even though this was the expected behaviour of the ideal official),

and books burned under China's First Emperor

BY PERMISSION OF THE BRITISH LIBRARY 74.D.45 WI5

but by couching their criticism in historical terms they might avoid present punishment while fulfilling their Confucian duty. If their advice was rejected, or if they were exiled or demoted, they could compare themselves to Qu Yuan and gain solace from the belief that history would judge them favourably. Such an allusion would imply that, although the emperor might be a good ruler, he was misguided and had been given poor advice by others.

Political careers in imperial China, even the most successful, were usually punctuated by periods of exile, demotion or worse. Deng Xiaoping's three banishments into the political wilderness continue this tradition. The official who supported the students in 798 was himself banished seven years later. On passing the Miluo River he wrote the obligatory poem, in this case entitled 'Mourning Qu Yuan':

I am saddened that those in office today have no concerns with the good and evil of the time.
They only fear that their salaries are too low, or that they may not be promoted.
I walk silently by myself as my opinions were ignored.
Since dishonourable ways cannot be removed, I lament that the world forgets you.

Qu Yuan remains an iconic figure in China. It is not surprising that in June 1989 after the violent suppression of demonstrators in Beijing and other cities throughout China, students in Changsha made the following speech at a meeting to mourn the dead:

Was it the indignant, still-beckoning spirit of Qu Yuan from more than 2,000 years ago that took you away? Was it the heroic spirits of 70 years ago that called to you? Was it the loving heart of your numberless predecessors before the Monument to the People's Heroes that moved you so? You have gone, suddenly gone. You have left behind only a river of fresh blood, only a deep love and a deep hate. Spirits of Beijing, where do you rest? The mountains and rivers weep, the sad wind mourns. Before the muzzles of evil guns, before the ugly face of fascism, before our people in suffering and before your serene death mask, I can do no more than make this offering to your spirits.

You are gone. Today, 2,000 years ago, Qu Yuan, his heart afire with loyal ardour, leapt into the pitiless Miluo River. 'I submit to the crystal-clear depths,' he cried, 'Oh Death, come now!' Today, 2,000 years later, our loyal brothers and sisters fell under the guns of the so-called 'people's own soldiers'.

The written history of China has a small cast: the elite of educated men who yearned for an official career. Most never spoke out, but they saw themselves as belonging in a tradition of righteous criticism: the duty of every official when he saw the way of good government threatened. And he was well aware of the importance of history in preserving his deeds.

The vast majority of the population, the peasants, appear infrequently in this narrative. They have their own tradition of dissent, not expressed in fine words but by bloody rebellion. This, it has to be said, was often a lot more effective in ensuring the quick demise of the government. Chinese Communist historians in the 1950s and 1960s, praised these rebellions as examples of proto-Communist class struggle. Contemporary peasant riots against corruption, high taxes and lack of payment for state-sold grain, are now brutally suppressed. Instead of representing class-struggle, they are 'counter-revolutionary' movements. Similarly, workers' movements are only examples of revolutionary behaviour when they take place somewhere other than China. China's rulers today are as afraid of history being used to criticise their actions as were the First Emperor and his chief minister in the third century BC.

The continuity of the tradition of dissent is not matched by a continuity of totalitarianism. The burning of the books was not an isolated incident, but China's history of censorship is less severe than that of the Catholic Church. Political executions were not uncommon in China, but the legal code required that all capital cases be reviewed at several levels, ending with the emperor. Clemency was a sign of strength rather than weakness, and was commonly practised. In Elizabethan England, 20 or 30 men a day were hanged in London alone; China's Mongol emperors signed death warrants for hardly more than that every year.

China's Communist government therefore has its origins not in China's past, but in the totalitarian states of the twentieth century. Several of the Soviet Union's most disastrous policies were emulated by China. The mass collectivisation of farming which led to the Ukrainian famine was followed in China by the Great Leap Forward: 30 million starved. Stalin's political purge was followed in China by the Cultural Revolution. Mao's henchmen used the same methods of torture on his political enemies as those used on Stalin's. In these cases, China's leaders were well aware of the lessons of history, but chose to ignore them. As China experiences growing urbanisation and unfettered capitalism, it may be worth looking to nineteenth-century Britain for the lessons of history.

If the Chinese government hopes that urban life and improving living standards promised by the economic reforms will lessen the likelihood of protest, they should consider the words of a British historian on noting that urban workers were materially better-off compared to their rural grandparents: 'In such an age, the inequalities of life are apt to look less like calamities from the hand of heaven and more like injustices from the hand of man.' The official tally of over 6,000 strikes in China in 1993 indicates a dangerously high level of unrest in a country where protest can mean consignment to a labour camp or death.

Dissent, in words and actions, led to eventual reform in Britain. Chinese history offers a tradition of dissent. More recent European history offers modern Chinese dissidents hope for the future. ❏

Susan Whitfield *is head of the International Dunhuang Project at the British Library, London*

WANG DAN

Reflections on freedom

Mankind's age-old pursuit of freedom has always been bedevilled by the plethora of competing definitions of the object of his quest.

These encompass wildly different views, from those inspired by the negative capability embodied in the laws of physics or the theory of freedom elaborated around the economic concept of 'marginal utility value' to that most commonly quoted — the limits of my freedom are determined by your interests.

One way of working through the confusion is to determine what constitutes a complete *lack* of freedom — as, for instance, censorship defines the absence of free expression. Only by pinning things down in a practical way does theory keep in touch with reality and stand a chance of coming up with solutions to our problems rather than indulging in idle prattle.

The German philosopher Hegel made a mockery of freedom when he claimed that 'freedom is understanding the inevitable.' It was precisely this that led Hegel to place the will of the state above that of the individual, a theory adopted by facism and the sworn enemy of freedom. Hegel's doctrine assumes there are higher demands within freedom and that mankind should sacrifice freedom in response to the demands of the state. But freedom is the highest value in human consciousness. Its only restrictions stem from within freedom itself.

Man's material and spiritual needs are many and varied, often without tangible form. What they have in common, over and above apparent contradictions, is their pursuit of a common goal, freedom. One way of entering this realm is through literature. Whether writing or reading, people invest something of themselves, their feelings, into a literary work. By giving vent to something within, they gain a sense of freedom. The same can be said of imagination: close your eyes, allow your mind to wander,and you can set sail on a voyage across the oceans or gallop across the desert astride a horse. The fetters of the real world grow distant; the limitless freedom of the soul brings boundless happiness.

The pursuit of freedom has always been at the centre of human society, the motivating force behind social progress and evolution. In this context, even conventionally 'bad' behaviour may at times be motivated by the pursuit of freedom. For example, to achieve social standing, an individual may act unscrupulously, even endangering society as a whole. Yet the lure of higher social standing as a goal that will liberate him from the repression and restrictions of normal social conventions into a realm of opportunity and give him a greater sense of his own social and economic worth, represents for him the pursuit of greater freedom.

Economic theory tells us that the greater the consumption of any given commodity, the less the satisfaction of the consumer and vice versa. What does it tell us of freedom? That a surfeit of freedom lessens the appetite? The converse is certainly true: when an individual or society has been totally deprived of freedom, a single drop will raise it to a state of euphoria.

The application of this theory helps explain the present situation in China where, paradoxically, the granting of limited political freedoms is accompanied by muted waves of popular protest. By comparison with the Cultural Revolution, freedoms have increased somewhat. In the eyes of a people whose freedoms have been consistently curtailed, this increase gives rise to a sense of blind satisfaction. However, further increases in freedom will lead to growing secret dissatisfaction.

The most popular understanding of freedom in circulation today defines it as doing whatever one pleases without infringing the rights of others. In other words, freedom is not absolute.

This is somewhat misleading. Some freedoms, such as freedom of thought, are purely internal and, therefore, absolute. We cannot speak of freedom and restriction in the same breath. Restricting freedom does not prevent its abuse; nor is the fear of abuse a legitimate reason for denying freedom. The proper exercise of freedom must be allied with responsibility.

Civilised society opposes the abuse of freedom, but this has nothing to do with the fundamental suppression of freedom in autocratic societies. Freedom is linked to responsibility: exercising the right to freedom assumes social and legal responsibilities. Democracy and the rule of law are as inseparable as are autocracy, dictatorship and [our] government.

Beijing Spring *New York, 1995*

Wang Dan*, a student leader prominent in the 1989 democracy movement, was sentenced to 11 years' imprisonment in October 1996*
Translated by Desmond Skeel

JASPER BECKER

How to say no

IN the dreary and regimented world of Chinese publishing, *China Can Say No — Political and Sentimental Options in the Post Cold War Era* has exploded like a firework.

The blunt, caustic and nationalistic polemic reflects the gut feelings of many of China's post-Tiananmen youth. Over 100,000 copies were sold in the first month turning its authors into celebrities. The rambling, sometimes witty and often contradictory rants mirror what the rebellious students of the 1980s now feel: veiled dissatisfaction with the government, anger and disappointment with the USA and a growing pride in China's achievements.

The book was written in three weeks by five authors: Zhang Xiaobo (penname Zhang Zang Zang), Song Qiang, Qiao Bian and two others not named, and published in May last year.

Zhang and Song are now 32 and were classmates at the East China Normal University in Shanghai. Neither are Party members although Song was once a member of the Youth League and now claims to be a Buddhist. Song is a producer at a local radio station in Chongqing, his home town, and graduated in Chinese Literature. Zhang resigned from a job at the Chinese Cultural and Art Federation to set up his own company which is currently launching a series of translations of modern French literature. A pugnacious fast talking poet, Zhang has published both verse and fiction including his latest novel *The River that Drowns One Child Each Day*.

The runaway success of the book encouraged many other copycat works so the authors promptly wrote another called *China Can Still Say No*, later in the same year. This directs the brunt of its anger against Japan. The authors compare the erection of the lighthouse on the Diaoyu Island — ownership of which is disputed by China and Japan — by Japanese extremists to Hitler's annexation of the Ruhr which set Germany on the road to military expansion.

It says China must protect the islands and attacks Chinese diplomacy for being too weak willed. It demands instead some forceful 'people's diplomacy' with mass actions by all kinds of groups.

'Diplomacy should not only be about the doings of experts, its priority must be to safeguard national interest,' the book says and continues belligerently: 'The "gentlemen" will wring their eyebrows and comment with a sigh that "it will worsen Sino-Japanese relations." But what is the priority in such times — respect and posterity, or short term economic and trade interests? We can separate the Chinese into two camps: the pure Chinese and the turncoat Chinese who become traitors at the drop of a hat.'

This sort of ludicrous posturing would be fun if it were not for the fact the authors clearly have official backing from the top of the Communist Party. In a country which under Mao (and many emperors before him) revelled in a dangerous and violent xenophobia, these attitudes inspire alarm among foreign diplomats.

It also evokes a kind of disgust among Chinese who see these young intellectuals being used as pawns by more dangerous and cynical leftists who are now trying to drive China back to an earlier era. The liberals believe it would be better for young Chinese to distrust their elders in the Party a little more rather than seeking to blame foreigners for their country's ills. ❏

'Knives and forks are backward and primitive. Long ago, after our ancestors learned to use iron, they cut animal flesh into pieces with knives, roasted the meat and picked it up with forks... In contrast, it is quite another thing to use chopsticks: it requires people to co-ordinate their hands and fingers with skill. To some extent it is a sort of art and a symbol of yearning for peace'

China Can Say No

Jasper Becker *is the Beijing correspondent for the* South China Morning Post. *He is the author of* Hungry Ghosts *(John Murray, 1996; paperback due in March 1997)*

China Can Say No

Cover, Beijing edition of China Can Say No

ON BRITAIN

WHEN Prime Minister John Major came to China for the signing ceremony of the agreement to build Hong Kong's new airport, he told Premier Li Peng in an overbearing way: 'Before I left Britain, I received a letter from some Labour Party politicians who asked me to raise human rights issues with you.' Premier Li Peng replied cleverly but forcefully: 'I also received letters from some Chinese historians. They go like this: we shall never forget that China was once bullied by western powers for over 100 years and we haven't settled accounts over their violation of Chinese human rights during that period!'

As the earliest and biggest drug dealer in the whole world, Britain launched the 'Opium War' to protect its 'right' to dump opium in China. Can time ever erase such a terrible human rights record?.. In the history of mankind, the Opium War is the only example of such a devastating war being waged for such shameful business.

Let's look at how western countries became rich: gentlemanly Britain did it by selling opium and thus can be classified as the biggest drug dealer in modern history... First a drug dealer, then a war monger. To sell its opium more effectively, Britain sent its expeditionary forces in the name of justice. It even demanded respect from others. I believe that the superiority complex, pride and prejudice in the attitude of some westerners toward the Chinese stemmed from the defeat of the central empire.

ON HONG KONG

1 JULY 1997 is getting close. After being 'rented' for one and a half centuries, Hong Kong is coming back to the Motherland. As the first and most miserable page full of humiliation and mishaps in China's modern history, Hong Kong teaches us many things that we shall never forget.

Britain is still making trouble over Hong Kong on the sly.

China rebuffed drug dealers with a clear 'NO' when Liu Tse-hsu openly dumped 2,000 tons of opium into a pit of quick lime in the spring of 1939... On the eve of Hong Kong's return, Chinese people will say 'No' loud and clear to those who try to divide China.

HONG Kong's return is not all sweetness and light. While we are joyfully counting down to the final second, the last colonial government in Hong Kong is busy squandering money like a dishonest contractor. It reminds me of the words of Louis XIV: '*Après moi le déluge*'... Everyone knows the real reason for Britain's hasty decision to confer 'democracy' on Hong Kong. Compare it with its behaviour when quitting India and Pakistan. This time its effort will be in vain. (*China Can Still Say No*)

ON TIBET

I'M astonished that the American media can be so absurd and misguided as to ignore the fact that the Chinese central government is providing massive help to the Tibetan people. It shows their ignorance of geo-economic matters.

The so-called human rights issue in Tibet is a constant topic in the annual human rights reports published by the US Congress. Comments on the situation in Tibet in its 1995 edition are frequently prefaced by phrases such as 'it is said', 'according to reliable reports' or 'according to reliable sources'; they seize on one point and ignore the overall picture.

The report is full of contradictions: it criticises the Chinese government for its failure to improve the living standards of Tibetan people and at the same time slanders the massive construction works in Lhasa and other areas that [it says] are destroying the unique culture there. This is a clear demonstration that one can always trump up a charge if one is out to condemn someone.

To Americans, there are no better ways of containing China than splitting it up so that it won't have the time to attend to its economic development. Their current actions, such as claiming Tibet as a 'sovereign state' and even passing bills in their Congress to send special envoys to Tibet, stem from the same motives that led them, in the 1950s, to train Tibetan rebels and equip them with arms to destabilise China's Tibetan area. When looking into the past, we discovered that the Soviet Union used the same method with Outer Mongolia. By encouraging it to seek independence, the USSR succeeded in forcing China to cede over one million square kilometres of land, and eventually turned Outer Mongolia into its own dependency... US attempts to impede China's economic development by making trouble in China over Tibetan issues are doomed to failure.

'In major diplomatic crises, China should sometimes have the courage and ambition to push aside the United States'

ON TRADE AS A WEAPON

WHEN Premier Li Peng visited France, he signed lots of purchase contracts despite the resentment of the British and Americans. I fully support this. I am very much in favour of China's political decision to do business with western countries: don't tell me that 'politics and business don't mix' because the maxim certainly doesn't apply to western politicians. In my view, competition between western countries for our market gives us the opportunity to put 'the spirit of Macmillan' — a former British foreign minister who said 'there are no eternal friends only eternal interests' — into practise... The cancellation of contracts is the best medicine to cure those obstinate western powers of their conviction that only they are in the right.

Faced with the possibility of US trade retaliation, Wu Yi, the woman who is our foreign trade minister, understood exactly how to handle the situation. Far from being intimidated, the Chinese 'iron lady' gave the Americans a stern warning: 'We will announce our counter-retaliation measures as soon as you announce your sanctions.' Wu Yi put investment restriction on the Chinese list. It hit home in the USA because at that precise moment General Motors was going all out for joint venture with China.

'America can lead nobody but itself; Japan can lead nobody, sometimes not even itself; China does not want to lead anyone, it only wants to lead itself'

China's use of the investment card was effective: despite strong pressure from the major US entrepreneurs, US trade representatives made no more excessive demands... Once the two sides had signed their agreement, Wu Yi and Charlene Barshefsky held a press conference. All the journalists present were full of admiration for Wu Yi who had dared to say 'No' to America. She represents the modern China that is determined to safeguard its own interests and pride in defiance of foreign powers.

America can contain China economically; China can do the same to America. You do as you please; we Chinese can play by our own rules... The contract for Airbuses for China provides jobs for many Frenchmen... It [also] shows the Americans that Boeing is not the only aircraft manufacturer... If the US government wields its big trade stick, China has other options... China can close the door of its market to anyone who tries to block the development of the Chinese economy. ❏

From China Can Say No *(China United Industrial and Commercial Press, Beijing 1996) and its sequel* China Can Still Say No

Translated by Ma Jun

CHEN XIAOMING

False dawn

Those who set out to avoid politics end up in accord with official ideology

THE huge upsurge in nationalist feeling and the rapidly expanding influence of the far right, typified at its most populist level by the best-seller, *China Can Say No,* demonstrate the strong cultural forces at work in China today.

The main cultural trends of the eighties were 'anti–traditional' and favoured 'total westernisation'; yet only a few years into the 1990s Chinese national culture and vigorous calls for resistance against western 'Imperialist Powers' are back in vogue.

While they appear contradictory, the ideological trends of the 1980s and 1990s can be traced to the same source. In the 1980s, 'traditional Chinese culture' was blamed for any problem encountered in China's modernisations. Come the 1990s, 'the West's containment of China' has become the scapegoat for China's own internal political and cultural tensions as well as continuing concerns about modernisation.

By the late 1980s, Chinese ideology had become fragmented: officials, intellectuals and ordinary people no longer shared common ground. 'Patriotism' has become the official unifying ideology of the 1990s.

It would be unrealistic to suggest that ordinary people and intellectuals identified themselves with patriotism independently. In the case of the intellectuals, it was more a matter of retreating into traditional scholarship to avoid any particular political stance. After the events of 1989, academics realised that continued advocacy of western learning would be problematic, hence the expedient 'return to traditional Chinese scholarship', justified as an academic pursuit, a retreat from the exciting, but meaningless history of thought to calm and solid research into the history of scholarship.

Ironically, those who had set out to avoid politics ended up in accord

'Spring is not far away.' New sculpture by Huang Yongyu

with official ideology. It became the norm to revere the modern masters of Chinese traditional scholarship and such notions as 'only the Chinese can engage in meaningful research into Chinese matters'; calls for 'a return to traditional standards', and the 'rebuilding of Chinese academic standards' became popular topics of conversation giving rise to ideas such as 'the nativisation of social sciences', 'anti-modernisation', 'the specific characteristics of the Chinese way' and 'the twenty–first century belongs to the Chinese', notions that are transformed into the noisy polemic of *China Can Say No.*

Ordinary people remained indifferent to all this, much as they had to earlier calls for westernisation: historically, the aspirations of the Chinese have always been determined and articulated by politicians and intellectuals. However, in the 1990s, as the economy expanded, ordinary people also started to believe the fairy tale that 'the twenty–first century belongs to the Chinese.' Those businessmen who have benefited most from the introduction of foreign capital following economic liberalisation are particularly wedded to this fantasy. In the Special Economic Zones (SEZs) and cities of the coastal areas of south China it is not difficult to find rich businessmen who are enthusiastic proponents of traditional culture, their nationalist leanings already entrenched in the management structure of their enterprises and corporate strategy.

While it is easy to explain the shift of intellectuals and the business community, the young poets and journalists who suddenly exhibited an extreme nationalism are a different proposition. In the 1980s, these people were keen advocates of westernisation and there are still one or two 'poets' among them preoccupied with western notions such as 'individualism' and 'personal freedom'. Why are the majority convinced that they were wrong in the past, but right today? Some say they are motivated solely by money: profitability has become the supreme value; 'success' means economic success.

The loss of spiritual values has made the '30-something' generation even more pragmatic when dealing with ideology and selecting values. The call to 'oppose western imperialist hegemony' has filled the vacuum left by the collapse of faith and given rise to cultural pride and vanity.

Despite their lack of experience, those carrying the banner of patriotism became veteran politicians overnight. These 'latter–day Red Guards' are powerfully in the ascendant, promoting extreme nationalism under the banner of patriotism; giving ultra–right expression to the left-wing attitudes that have always existed in Chinese society.

The extreme tendencies of today's nationalism could become a double-edged sword. China is at a cross-roads and needs the full support of the international community. We must not assume we have unlimited capital to squander. Saying 'no' may be gratifying — in the last century or more China has frequently said 'no': our 'nos' throughout the 1950s and 1960s cost us many opportunities. It is by no means a foregone conclusion that the twenty–first century belongs to the Chinese. And it certainly will not come about from saying 'no'. ❏

Chen Xiaoming is an academic with the Academy of Social Sciences, Beijing

Translated by Janine Nicol

ISABEL HILTON

Han rejects

The government's patriotic nationalism bodes ill for China's minorities, especially in Tibet

IN Beijing it is fashionable once again to attribute China's ills to the excesses of western influence, a device that can be relied upon to awaken some response in the Han population of China and distract attention from the real issues: the legitimacy of the current regime and its legion of corrupt cadres. But on the fringes of the People's Republic, in the remote regions of Xinjiang, Mongolia and Tibet, to blame the legacy of colonialism as the main problem strikes a different note: there, the experience of colonialism is altogether fresher and the colonial power is not perceived as western, but as Han Chinese. In China's minority areas, Chinese nationalism has hit this year at different targets — at the traditional religious and national feelings that have, if Beijing's propaganda is to be believed, undergone such a vigorous revival that they pose an ideological and political threat to the dominance of Beijing.

As *China Can Say No* was enjoying its post-publication success in the cities of the east, Abdulahat Abdurixit, the chairman of the Xinjiang Uighur Autonomous Regional People's Government was reporting on the campaign, by then several months long, against 'separatism' in Xinjiang, and the success of the 'strike hard' campaign (see *Index* 4/1996)

The campaign was presented as a crackdown on crime, but in Tibet its political purpose became clear when the *Tibet Daily* announced that it should include a campaign against pro-independence forces loyal to the Dalai Lama, with the death penalty imposed whenever warranted. A series of minor explosions were laid at the door of the Dalai Lama and provided the excuse for an attempt to eradicate his influence and his image. In May, police attempts to remove his photograph, in compliance with a new order from Beijing, sparked off a riot in Ganden monastery,

TIBET INFORMATION NETWORK/TIN

Kumbum monastery, Qinghai, China 1995: monastery school closed and students arrested in May 1996 after distributing posters urging Tibetan independence

25 miles east of Lhasa that resulted, according to the Tibet Information Network (TIN), in one child monk being shot by police and a further 80 people being injured, 30 of them women. Following the clash most monasteries around Lhasa were sealed off.

The campaign of vilification of the Dalai Lama has reached a new pitch in the last six months. After the May disturbances, there was further trouble in August with the beginning of a re-education campaign in the monasteries in the style of the Cultural Revolution. Its aim was to identify and eliminate dissent and to force the religious sector to conform to Beijing's new rule: that the first duty of any religion was patriotism.

It began in the troublesome Ganden monastery where around 150 monks, according to TIN, were expelled at the end of August for 'going against the nation', charges that appear to have arisen from the May disturbances and from the failure of some monks to give the right answers in a written examination in which they were asked to write down the four 'crimes' of the Dalai Lama. From Ganden it spread to the other main monasteries of Tibet. According to TIN, one monk in Drepung monastery, six kilometres west of Lhasa, was given a three-year prison sentence for contradicting the claim of the political educators that Tibet had been part of China since the thirteenth century. Four others are in custody with unknown sentences.

Nine monks have been arrested from Sera monastery, three kilometres north of Lhasa, apparently after being found with leaflets, literature or posters which criticised the re-education process and at Sakya monastery, 100 kilometres southwest of Shigatse, a monk died in the local county prison on 14 September, two weeks after being arrested during a re-education session.

On 8 November, the secretary of the Chinese Communist Party in Tibet, Chen Kaiyuan, made a speech to his party in which he summed up the situation in Tibet after the first three months of the rectification campaign. The content of Chen Kaiyuan's speech is sobering to those with an interest in the future of Tibetan culture in Chinese hands. Tibet has been under Chinese control for nearly half a century during which time the Chinese ambition to achieve the 'socialist transformation' of Tibet's traditional culture has gone through varying degrees of virulence. Now, with the rest of China given over to rapid economic development and with nationalism as the dominant political mode in Beijing, Tibet is suffering a drive for ideological purity of a virulence not seen for nearly

20 years. The essential problem remains, as Chen Kaiyuan's speech makes clear, the Tibetan attachment to Buddhism and the position of the Dalai Lama. But this, according to a number of official pronouncements on Tibet in recent months that chime closely with the thinking behind *China Can Say No*, conceals a more sinister hand: 'Western forces,' one recent official statement said, 'want to use Tibet as a breakthrough point and are trying every way to contain us and obstruct and sabotage our country's socialist modernisation drive.' Or, as Chen Kaiyuan put it, 'the splittist forces with Dalai [sic] as the leader propagate the thinking of "Tibet Independence" [and] create the public opinion of splittism and instigate disturbances by using religious influences with western media as a main channel and monasteries as key positions.'

The problem is not just inside the monasteries. He goes on: 'Affected by splittist forces, Tibetan Buddhism experiences malignant expansion in the negative side, its purpose and doctrine are distorted and Buddhist disciplines are violated. Religious believers, and even some party members and cadres are not able to free themselves from the shackles of their outlook on the world as seen from religious idealism. Instead of devoting their intelligence and endeavours to the welfare of society and the people, they waste their precious time in futile financial resources to improve their economic condition, they unrestrictedly donate their money to monasteries; and instead of letting their children receive modern education, they send them to monasteries to become a monk or a nun.' 'Old customs', he complains have returned and outmoded beliefs are harming the advance of science and spiritual civilisation.

Old customs, including religious customs, have undergone a considerable revival all over the People's Republic in the last decade: some of them, like Confucianism, have been welcomed by the authorities as both an affirmation of Asian civilisation and a convenient tool to enhance social order. But Tibetan 'old customs' are apparently a different matter: the impact of them, Chen Kaiyuan argues, is 'very serious'. So while Han China can practice Confucianism, Daoism and even Chinese Buddhism, in Tibet the solution proposed is 'ideological development' with 'patriotism and socialism' as the core beliefs. Party members, he said, must 'disseminate the truth that only socialism can save and develop Tibet.' ❏

Isabel Hilton is a writer and broadcaster. She is currently writing a book on the Panchen Lama

New censors

After the Party's Central Committee's Sixth Plenary in October, the Central Propaganda Department promulgated eight new regulations prohibiting the media from reporting on anything that might damage the image of the Party or government or affect the political stability of the country. Observers say that censorship is currently stronger than at any time since the Cultural Revolution. The regulations are:

• In order to guarantee unity of thinking and to avoid a negative impact on political stability, all sensitive issues, such as the campaign to protect the Daiyou Islands or the overseas democracy movement, are not to be covered.
• All cases which have a significant impact or wide involvement should not be reported, such as the case of the former secretary of the Beijing Municipal Committee, Chen Zitong, or the case of Zhou Beifang of the Capital Iron and Steel Works.
• There have been over 10,000 cases of demonstration and protests in the urban and rural areas within this past year. All of these are not to be covered.
• Articles written by dissidents are not to be published.
• Propaganda departments of different levels must strengthen censorship over the media and deal with problems promptly.
• Propaganda departments of different levels must strengthen supervision over publication units; those that violate the regulations must be dealt with severely.
• When reporting on issues concerning Hong Kong, the media must act in accordance with the policy formulated by the Party Central Committee.
• When reporting on foreign affairs, the media must not reveal state secrets.

Excerpted from China Focus, *December 1996*

AND YOU THOUGHT IT WASN'T 1997 YET!

Soft on China Morning Post

LARRY FEIGN

FEIGN

Unofficial magazines in China 1988-1995

Title	Publication
The Nineties	12/1989 – 3/1993
Tropic of Cancer	12/1988 – 8/1993
TendencyQuarterly	Spring 1988 – Summer 1996
Discovery	12/1990 – 12/1992
Dissent	1/1990 – 7/1993
Modern Chinese Poetry	Spring 1991 – Summer 1994
Southern Poetry Magazine	Autumn 1992 – Autumn 1993
Poetic Art	Spring 1993 – Spring 1994
Fantasy	Volumes 6&7, 5/1993
Composition	10/1992 – 12/1993
Superficial Reflections/Return	1/1993 – 3/1994
Superficial Reflections	10/1994
Poetry	Spring 1994
Orthodoxy	6/1994
Tumult	12/1991 – 4/1994
Voices	Summer 1992 – Autumn 1994
The Bird	Spring 1992 – Autumn 1994to
Words and Voices	Autumn 1994
The Front	8/1994
The Others	Winter 1994
Transition	Winter 1991 – Autumn 1994
Connection	1/1995
Apollinaire	Spring 1995
North Gate Magazine	Summer 1995
The Sunflower	10/1991 – 8/1992
Stranger	Spring 1990 – Spring 1992
Lucky Survivor	7/1988 – Winter 1989
Condition	Winter 1992
Xiang Wang	10/1989 – 2/1992

Dates listed do not necessarily represent either the number of issues published during this time, nor the end of a title. Publication is, in most cases, irregular: some magazines may have ceased publication; others may still be available. The table represents our knowledge at the time of going to press

Editors	Place
Xiao Kaiyu	Chengdu
Meng Lang, Liang Xiaoming et al	Hangzhou
Chen Dongdong, Bei Ling et al	Beijing/Shanghai
Zang Di, Xi Du, Ge Mai	Beijing
Xiao Kaiyu, Sun Wenpo	Chengdu
Mang Ke, Tang Xiaodu,	Beijing/Shanghai/
Meng Liang *et al*	Hangzhou/Shenzhen
Chen Dongdong	Shanghai
Wang Ai	Shenzhen/Wuhan
Zhou Lunyou, Ye Zhou	Beijing
Liu Junyi	Beijing
Xiang Zi, Jiang Cheng	Guangzhou
Jiang Cheng	Guangzhou
Chang Zheng, Pu Min, *et al.*	Jinan
Xia Zhihua, Jiang Xi	Nanjing
Wang Qiang, Wang Qiuren et al	Beijing/Guiyang
Huang Canran et al	Shenzhen/Hong Kong/Guangzhou
Shen Wei	Urumqi
Han Bo	Shanghai
Sen Zi, Geng Zhanchun	Henan
Han Dong, Yu Jian	Nanjing
He Bailun, Gang Ke	Harbin
Zhu Zhu	Nanjing
Pai Si	Hangzhou
Pang Pei	Jiangsu/Jiang Yin
Xiao Chen	Tianjin
Nan Fang	Shanghai
Yang Lian, Mang Ke, Xue Di,	Beijing
Tang Xiaodu, Lin Mang	
Zeng Hong, Zhuo Meihui,	Fuzhou
Yang Xuefan	
Zhong Ming, Zhao Ye,	Chengdu
Xiang Yichun, Chen Zihong, *et al*	

Source: Tendency Quarterly
Translated by Jenny Putin

YANG LIAN

Market lines

Money's the name of the game as one-time poets turn out politically acceptable nostalgia and erotica for the popular taste

'IN CHINA, we can write whatever we want.' The words are Yu Hua's. No, he is not a functionary in the Chinese Communist Party's Propaganda Department. He is the author of the popular story on which Zhang Yimou based his recent film, *To Live*. Yu Hua has just published four volumes of his collected writings, and belongs to what is known on the Chinese mainland as the 'avant-garde' school of writers. His remarks were based on the print-runs of his books' multiple editions, running into hundreds of thousands, and on the publishers and booksellers queuing up for his new work. 'The authorities,' he said, 'cannot control the market.' For writers and artists in mainland China today, what is 'real' is determined by what it can rake in; big sales amount to 'freedom'.

The market or, to put it plainly, money, defines the 'spirit of the age' in 1990s China. The aims of real dissidence or the exploration of new ways of thinking during the 1980s have, today, been deflected and turned into ways of making money. In order to attract and satisfy their customers — both eastern and western — artists have emerged from their once lonely, sometimes dangerous, pursuit of artistic form to become noisy, commonplace hawkers and stall holders. Whether it is the universally recognised brands of 'Chinese art': Mao's portrait, artifacts from the Cultural Revolution, new perversions of Chinese sexuality, ancient pseudo-exotica and so on, dressed up in cobbled-together critical jargon and presented as if they amounted to a 'unique, original' artistic language, or the literary realm, the features are much the same.

In Wang Shuo's highly popular and cleverly written literary memoirs, the Cultural Revolution has become an object of nostalgic connoisseurship. The depiction of the traditional Chinese family in Su

Tong's *Wives and Concubines* (which Zhang Yimou filmed as *Raise the Red Lantern*) allows his readers to enjoy vicarious voyeuristic delights. Women writers untiringly and incessantly trample themselves underfoot, while male authors, such as Jia Ping'ao, write tales of the capital's urban decadence where the only things that don't decay are food and sex — his sure-fire popularity plays on the constant hunger, thirst and desires of a billion people. And then there is the contemporary clamour of the 'avant-garde', who ridicule themselves in the words of their own 'avant-garde theorist', Chen Xiaoming, 'Chinese critics discuss Chinese writers, while Chinese writers discuss foreign writers.' These days, the advance of a few thousand pounds is enough to seduce a fine young writer of love poetry into accepting any order to turn out, say, an erotic novel or an annotated edition of Chairman Mao's traditional poetry.

THE huge differences between the spirit of the age today, and that during the 'awakenings' and 'reconsiderations' of the 1980s are amazing. As someone who was part of it, I recognise an almost comical relationship between the two periods. The 'reconsideration' of the 1980s was not a quest for self-realisation. It was an oppressively conditioned response to the painful stimulus of the Cultural Revolution. In 1989 the sounds of gunfire on Tiananmen Square wrote a blank space in the minds of Chinese intellectuals who had long hoped to achieve power through knowledge — the century-old dream of 'saving the nation with culture' was finally found to be less powerful than a bullet. Naked power, in its extreme moments, has no need of intellectual knowledge, and no concern for 'thought'. Beneath the imported vocabularies of 'socialism' and 'capitalism', the pragmatic exercise of power is its only truth. 'Pragmatism', or, we might also say pure, unconstrained 'desire', allows unprincipled power and intellectually heedless money to share our lowest common denominator. The 'Cultural Revolution of Cash' during which 'everybody plunged into profit-taking' after 1992, took its slogans from Wang Shuo's street-wise novels: 'There are no rules, none at all.' 'Get hooked first, then die.' [The popular phrases *'Jinqian wenhua geming'*, literally 'Money Cultural Revolution' and *'quanmim xiahai'*, literally, 'the whole people plunges into the sea', meaning to take the necessary risks and throw yourself into business.] Mirror-like, these slogans reinforce the ways of thinking propagated by power in China. The 'musts' of the 1980s' reconsiderations have been easily abandoned. There has been a move

HUANG YONGYU

The cat: 'Using your tongue to clean yourself began with me'

from enforced thought to 'actively' *not* thinking and, finally, to the point where the cash value replaces the value of any thought.

The bases of democratic society — individual self-determination and self-knowledge — far from being strengthened, are abolished by the inundation of the market. The market proposes and cultivates a cadre of risk-taking entrepreneurs willing to pursue wealth by whatever means. Yet theirs is not a 'free' market. To disregard convention, to fail, moreover, to preserve and affirm the existing framework of power — this is as difficult in China as trying to break into Heaven. For example, there would be a huge market in direct political criticisms. But to enter that market would be to enter a minefield. Even a personal memoir, like Jung Chang's *Wild Swans*, is currently banned. On the one hand there are the prison doors of political crime, on the other, the seductive temptations of money. The 'popular taste' of a market 'with Chinese characteristics' has combined with the flattering, seductive 'charm' of contemporary artistic pragmatism. Unfortunately, sales increase in proportion to the loss of the individual self. The fact is, when one eagerly enters this (ideologically

TANG XIAODU

Survivors

The poet is a survivor, transcending language to enter the individual world of creation. Not the simple reproduction of work that has been, nor the romantic pursuit of what is to come, but excavating, unifying and elevating language; charging into unknown realms of life and giving them form. The birth of a poem is like the recreation of the world; language is the poet's only way of survival.

For the poet or the artist, survival presents no choice in the usual sense of the word. The creation of poetry and art is the only thing he can do. Only through this does their survival gain meaning, acquire respect. And at times, led by chance, he will create the songs within the poems.

Tang Xiaodu is the editor of Modern Chinese Poetry, *Beijing*

Translated by Oliver Kramer

controlled) market-place — itself characterised by a particular politics and marketable taste — the underlying message of any success you achieve is that you have succeeded in joining a particular ideology. The silent acquiescence of the authorities and the abandonment of individuality by artists — power and money — form a perfect union, an unholy edifice, which can only give rise to what the Chinese people have satirised as 'the worst of socialism combined with the worst of capitalism'. So, I am forced to call it a 'New Official Culture', a culture that has been bought out by the authorities.

There is nothing unusual in this. The structure of traditional Chinese society was one in which the state gathered central power, and the people went about their private business; the less constrained play of instinct and sensuality (food, sex, gambling, etc) was tacked onto this basic structure. The 'reforms' of the 1990s simply take the Chinese people *back* to their old ways and attitudes — although without the substantive framework of the traditional culture. This much is certain: 20 years after the Cultural Revolution, no significant and important literary works have emerged.

Writers do not dare discuss politics critically, but everywhere, they quietly project the prevailing politics through their work. Most recently, since there is no more 'politics', there is no more literature; apart, that is, from a large stack of contentious works which suggest content but have no form, which have superficial plots and no point to them, which have 'events but no people' — so-called real life experiences of deep hurt and hidden torment that never achieve any measure of 'profundity'. I think of it as 'a landscape lacking the eyes to see it'. Before the end of the 1980s, the successful writers were in fact officials nurtured by the state; in the 1990s, the successful writers are those which, as Deng Xiaoping advised, 'add to the glory of the nation' and 'get rich first'. Apart from that of a few fine sensibilities, the 'living knowledge' displayed in the work of contemporary Chinese writers is almost inconceivably meagre. It's not that all signs of the Cultural Revolution have disappeared; the political jargon of that era has now inspired real signs above fashionable restaurants everywhere with names like 'The Class of '66-'68', 'Black Earth', 'Rusticated Youth'. So now you can eat and drink the Cultural Revolution. It's as simple as that: the history of that time is forgotten, among this generation of ours that thought so highly of itself!

IN the last analysis, it is not that autocratic power either condones or suppresses art, it is the individuated originality of artistic form and content which has no means of condoning autocracy. Artists must acknowledge and accept their fate. In stark contrast with the glossy, highly publicised productions of the 'New Official Literature', 1991 saw the publication of an important new poetry magazine, *Modern Chinese Poetry*. Its style unavoidably recalled the publications of the 'Democracy Wall' period — coarse paper, mechanical typing and hand-made mimeography. And yet it made a deep impression on me, the most striking periodical of its kind I have seen. The work of performance artist Zhang Huan, '65 Kilos', provides another such contrast. He hung himself with hooks from a ceiling, naked, such that drops of his blood fell onto the bars of an electric fire, filling the air with a salty, fleshy haze. Another performance artist, Ma Liuming, in his piece, 'Lunch', slowly fried a fish outside, also naked, at 20 degrees below freezing, until the food became charcoal. These works are individual, they have their own language. Art has always been like this. The literary revelations of the late 1970s can be summed up in one simple sentence: 'Use your own language to describe your own experience.' In 1996, two Beijing artists' colonies, its own 'East Village' and 'West Village' were shut down, in sharp contradiction of this sentence. This brings us back to Yu Hua and what he said in Sweden. There, when he spoke with great erudition about the 'humorous relationship' between reality and the fictions of Kafka or Faulkner, did he also think that there was some sort of 'humorous' relationship between his own work and Chinese realities? Between authentic success — in literature, in art, in *humanity* — and success in this market, there is a small, but sharp, distinction. ❏

Yang Lian, a poet and critic from Beijing, was born in 1955. A number of his books were banned during the early months of 1987. He now lives in the UK. His most recent works are Non–Person Singular *(parallel text) and the poetic sequence* Where the Sea Stands Still *(Wellsweep Press)*

Translated by John Cayley, with the author

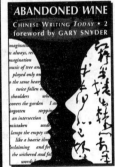

HAN DONGFANG

A voice for the millions

Industrial workers are the biggest losers in China's scramble for modernisation. Unemployment is growing, work conditions are appalling, strikes are commonplace. The exiled founder of China's independent labour movement sets the scene for future upheaval

AUGUST 14, 1993 is a day I shall always remember. On that day, five days before my thirtieth birthday, I was forcibly deported from my own country by the Chinese government. Neither will I forget the words of the policemen who escorted me over the Luo Wu bridge to the Hong Kong side of the border: 'People like you have no right to call yourselves Chinese.' In China we say 'Life begins at 30.'

Five days before my thirtieth birthday, when I was stripped of Chinese citizenship, I felt my life was ending.

IN 1989, I was employed as an electrical engineer on the railways. In May and June of that year, I and a number of fellow workers set up the Beijing Workers Autonomous Federation (BWAF), the first independent trade union in China since 1949. None of us had a clear idea about what an independent union should be doing. All we knew was why we needed one: the only official trade union, the All-China Federation of Trade Unions (ACFTU), is under the total control of government and Party: a department of government rather than a trade union. It has never achieved anything for Chinese workers and, if workers are to improve their conditions, we must have our own organisations. Once news of the BWAF spread, workers in other cities responded by setting up independent organisations.

It took the government only two weeks to suppress the BWAF. But even in this short time, we were able to give voice to the feeling of millions of Chinese workers who had been duped for too long by China's so-called politicians. For two weeks we were masters of our own destiny.

After the massacre on 4 June , the government relentlessly pursued and arrested all those who had taken part in autonomous trade unions. Pictures of myself and two colleagues were flashed across TV screens and newspapers nation-wide on the wanted list. Almost every street in China had a poster displaying our photographs, demanding that we be caught or turned in. Within a short time, most of us had been arrested and thrown into prison. I was tried and given a jail sentence of 22 months.

PRISON was the worst experience I have ever gone through. Routine beatings for ordinary prisoners are commonplace. If a prisoner breaks a rule, he is not allowed to talk to others, made to stand for at least 24 hours and deprived of sleep. Even for committing a trivial offence such as smoking a cigarette, a prisoner can be punished by having his hands tied behind his back for at least a week and sometimes for as long as two months. During this time, the convict is not allowed to eat with the other prisoners and has to take his food lying on the ground like a pig. If anyone helps him, not only is the length of the punishment doubled, the helper receives the same treatment. Even the minimum period of time for this punishment — a week — can leave the prisoner unable to move his hands from behind his back unless aided by others. He is left in acute pain and dependent on his fellow prisoners to pick things up for him and move his hands in front of him. The aim of such systematic punishment is to break the prisoners' spirit. To survive one must acknowledge one simple fact: human dignity can be arbitrarily humiliated.

For political prisoners, especially those who have attracted the attention of the international community, routine beatings are rare. I personally was neither beaten nor subjected to routine torture. But there are other ways of breaking the will of those who refuse to co-operate or admit their guilt.

For example, during my time in prison I became ill. The authorities interpreted my condition as part of my general refusal to co-operate and took me to a 'doctor' who inserted a 15 centimetre acupuncture needle into the palm of my hand. While moving the needle around inside my hand, the doctor explained that he had 'cured countless numbers of people in this place. It never takes more than one visit and they're cured.

I guarantee that after seeing me, you won't demand to see a doctor again.'

However, I continued to demand my basic right to legitimate medical treatment and as a result was placed in a cell no bigger than 14 square metres which contained 20 people, all of whom were suffering from infectious diseases — pulmonary tuberculosis, hepatitis, skin diseases and venereal diseases. The prison governor put me in the picture: 'So far we've been good to you, but you obviously don't know a good thing when you see it. You will soon see just how good to you we were being.' Fortunately, I only contracted hepatitis. Eventually, I had to have part of my right lung removed in the USA, but at least I was still alive.

A T the beginning of 1992, I was invited by the US trade union federation AFL-CIO and Human Rights Watch to go to the USA for medical treatment. I took advantage of my time abroad to publicise the independent trade union movement in China and the situation of Chinese workers.

On 13 August 1993, I arrived back in the southern Chinese city of Guangzhou and booked into a hotel. At six o'clock the next morning, police came crashing into my room and took me off to a police station. That afternoon, a police official formally explained: 'While receiving medical treatment abroad, you made speeches at international meetings in which you attacked the Chinese government. As such, you have seriously violated the Chinese constitution and are therefore to be exiled outside China's borders.' 'Tell me which law gives you the right to deport a Chinese citizen out of China?' I asked. 'We don't need laws,' he replied. 'We only follow orders.'

Since the 1989 clamp-down on autonomous trade unions, the situation of Chinese workers has deteriorated almost daily. Workers facing major industrial reforms have been left totally unprotected and, indeed, have become a target of the reform process. Meanwhile, those who are responsible for the huge losses in Chinese industrial enterprises continue to enjoy special treatment and privileges. Workers in foreign-invested enterprises (FIEs) often have to work in appalling conditions doing long hours of overtime with no guarantees on wages or health and safety. In response to the worsening situation, workers have taken various forms of action to protect their interests, including strikes and demonstrations, all of which have been at the instigation of workers themselves.

Hence the repeated attempts to set up independent trade unions. These

JULIO ETCHART

Shanghai Railway Station, 1996: migrant workers arrive from the countryside

include in 1992 the Free Labour Union of China (FLUC); efforts by the lawyer Zhou Guoqiang to print T-shirts demanding workers' rights to collective bargaining in 1994. Zhou and others also attempted to establish the League for the Protection of the Rights of Working People (LPRWP); and again in 1994, Li Wenming and others tried to set up the 'Workers Federation' for migrant workers in the Shenzhen Special Economic Zone (SEZ). Li is currently facing charges of 'government subversion' which carry a minimum sentence of 10 years and a maximum of life imprisonment. He has already spent 30 months in illegal detention.

The government's response has been severe repression. Nearly all those involved in attempts to establish independent unions have been arrested and are either in 'reform through labour' or 're-education through labour' camps. Zhou Guoqiang and Liu Nianchun were swiftly sentenced to three years 'reform through education' for trying to set up the LPRWP. Over 16 activists involved in organising the FLUC were sentenced to prison terms ranging from two to 20 years. Other workers involved in this case have been sentenced to three years' 're-education through labour'.

HISTORICALLY, China's trade union movement has always been the pawn of contending factions in their struggle for power. It has also been exploited by Triads or Mafia-type organisations. Aware of this history, the independent trade union movement has been at pains to separate itself from the struggle for political power. We want to serve as an opposition party tool and certainly not as a prop for the party in power. We aim to approach the problem of workers rights through collective bargaining and consultation with all players, including the government and industry.

Through this process, a politically independent trade union movement can make an enormous contribution to the democratisation of Chinese society. Once Chinese workers are given the opportunity to take part in decision making, and influence policies that affect their lives, there is a chance of breaking the traditional pattern of long periods of great suffering followed by the resort to violence to resolve political and social conflicts. This in turn will allow the fundamental reforms that Chinese society is currently going through to continue in a more stable climate.

For myself, I plan to stay in Hong Kong after the 1997 handover. The 'problem' of the Chinese working class is the most difficult and pressing question facing the government. In consequence, its fear of independent trade unions continues to grow. Despite the fact that we have repeatedly made it clear to the authorities that we are not anti-government, our very existence causes them great anguish and their attacks on us will become increasingly severe. ❏

Han Dongfang now lives in Hong Kong. He is the founder of China's banned independent labour movement and founding editor of the Hong Kong-based China Labour Bulletin
Translated by Tim Pringle

DIARY

JULIO ETCHART

Hide and seek

'*Baoqian, baoqian, wo buzhidao wo zuocuole shi!* Sorry! Sorry! I didn't know I was doing anything wrong!' I keep repeating, trying to get the intonation right while pointing at the Chinese in my phrase book.

Here I am, being arrested by the transport police for taking photographs outside Kunming railway station in Yunnan province. The officer in charge suddenly drops his impenetrable expression and bursts into uncontrollable laughter before finally settling into a more conciliatory mood, asking me to sit down and offering me a cup of green tea. I am finally allowed to leave after being warned not to document the situation of his fellow citizens again without seeking their permission first.

I have been photographing the hundreds of families of migrant workers from poor rural areas of the interior squatting outside the train and coach stations. They flock to the big cities and large provincial capitals in search of work in the thousands of new enterprise zones set up by the government. Guangdong, whose proximity to Hong Kong makes it attractive to foreign investors, is the biggest magnet for this huge internal exodus. Its Special Enterprise Zones (SEZs) house thousands of light industrial factories and assembly plants.

Rising unemployment and underemployment in China's countryside and in the shrinking state-run industries have created unprecedented social tensions. Urban unemployment is estimated to be at least 10 million, almost certainly well below the true figure, while an estimated 120 million 'surplus' workers live in rural areas. Hence China's massive internal migration, in particular the shift to the more prosperous coastal regions in the south and the east. There are an estimated 100 million migrant workers in China and a high proportion of Guangdong

Province's one million toy workers are migrants from central provinces.

After many days of negotiations in Hong Kong with managers and PR people from the main foreign-invested toy and electronic factories that operate on the mainland, I crossed the border with a colleague and interpreter from the Asia Monitor Resource Centre.

We can't believe our luck when the manager of the Apollo factory in Dongguan takes us for a tour of the installations and allows me to photograph the assembly line. I hear later that he was ticked-off by his boss in Hong Kong, who had apparently only agreed to our seeing the outside of the building.

Apollo is big on miniature animals and toy guns, but also on spray guns: the building is filled with the pungent smell of paint and a layer of oil fumes floats above the work benches. The ventilation is inadequate and very few workers are wearing masks or gloves.

Since it is impossible to talk to the employees while on duty, we wait outside for the shift to finish and go to a food stall nearby where we meet Yang Qintong, 17, a young woman from Gansu in northern China.

She's worked in electronic and plastic toy companies in Dongguan since 1994, and now works in the department making remote controls. Working hours are from 7.30am to 6.30pm for which Qintong earns about 350 Yuan a month (US$45). She earns an extra 10 Yuan (a little more than US$1) for three hours of overtime. Sometimes she manages to save some money to send back to her parents in Gansu. She longs to go back to her home village but has no idea what jobs are going back there.

After bluffing our way into another installation, an electronic toys assembly plant, and being denied access to two more, we went back to the border but not before checking out the bright lights of Shenzhen city. This boomtown opposite the new territories is growing at such an alarming speed that the whole place looks like a huge building site, and it is obvious that the infrastructure can't catch up with the dizzying pace of development. Open sewers and impassable muddy roads strewn with industrial litter greet us round every corner.

But the city's nouveau riche love the night life and we join a group of mobile-phone-ridden (one in each pocket, plus two pagers in the belt) limousine-driven entrepreneurs on a karaoke crawl around town. They seem to accept our disguise as procurement consultants for 'an important overseas company'.

It was an enlightening insight into the psychology of the New China.

Shenzen, 1996: workers dormitory outside the SEZ; Credit: Julio Etchart

The young elite has developed an insatiable appetite for western goods and the fast life and regard the migrant masses toiling for them in the factories as little better than animals. 'Those peasants are brutes. You have to whip them like donkeys to make them understand,' remarks Li Hao, general manager of a soft toys plant under contract to the 'Honey Kid' line after a few beers. Then picks up the microphone to slur through the last lines of 'My Way' in front of the karaoke screen.

We survive the outing and make it back to Hong Kong just before the border closure at midnight.

The following week we plan a special expedition to Bagualing, a large workers' dormitory outside Shenzhen. We don't bother to ask management for permission since we know they won't let us in. So it's pretty much a commando operation: in and out of each block of flats fast, pictures first, questions after — and pray the warden doesn't spot us. We interview a few workers before being evicted by two security guards. One who catches my imagination is squatting at the bottom of a bunk bed in a tiny room she shares with eight other young women. Her entire belongings are tidily arranged in one little corner of her nest. She is one of the millions of ants of this brave new world order.

Ling Tongang is a 17-year-old female worker from Sichuan province who came to work at the Laima Technologies electronics and toy factory; it manufactures walkie-talkies and portable communications equipment in Shenzhen SEZ. The pay is lower than she expected (about 400 Yuan a month: around US$55) and is not enough to save and send money home. About 70 Yuan a month (US$10) is deducted for food and lodging in the factory's dormitories. The hours are too long: night shifts are 10–11 hours and during peak season they do a 24-hour shift. Everyone is always tired.

We ask why the union does nothing to help them. She laughs and says, 'They are no good; they always side with management.' Will she stay on? 'Of course, if I find a better job I'll leave right away, but I can't do anything until then. I'm stuck here.' ❏

Julio Etchart is a UK-based photo-journalist. He visited Hong Kong and China in June-July 1996

TONY RAYNS

The well dries up

A YEAR is a long time in the Chinese film business. Much has changed for Chinese film-makers in the past 12 months (see *Index* 6/1995). Beijing's Ministry of Radio, Film and Television (MRFT) is finally implementing its new Film Administration Regulations: a 64-article tract which promises control, subsidy, protectionism and more control but contains nothing that will improve the quality, distribution, commercial viability or export potential of Chinese films — and nothing either to arrest the continuing sharp decline in Chinese film-going. These regulations will do little to win back or reassure the Hong Kong producers and Taiwanese financiers who have been propping up China's beleaguered

Banned in China: Gong Li in Chen Kaige's Temptress Moon *(1995)*

studios by masterminding 'co-productions'. In any case, these entrepreneurs have more pressing problems closer to home. Chinese-language films currently have a lower share of the Hong Kong market than at any time since the mid-1960s, and the audience in Taiwan appears to have lost all interest in seeing Chinese films. The coincidence of new political constraints in Beijing with box-office free-fall throughout the region has brought Chinese cinema to its lowest ebb in living memory.

Just two years ago it seemed plausible to suggest that Chinese cinema

TONY RAYNS

was in the process of erasing the political and cultural differences which had split the film industry into three strands some 45 years earlier. A film like Chen Kaige's *Farewell My Concubine* (1993) pointed the new way forward. Financed from Taiwan, produced from Hong Kong, shot in China by a mainland director and crew and with a cast drawn from all three territories, Chen's film not only proved that the three strands of Chinese cinema could work together but also showed they could come up with a film of strong global appeal. Sadly, that achievement seems unlikely to be matched any time soon, and not only because Chen's follow-up *Temptress Moon* (1996) has so far failed to duplicate the success of *Concubine*. The scope for co-operation in film production between China, Hong Kong and Taiwan is now extremely limited.

CHINA changed its top film bureaucrats at the start of 1996. The new minister for radio, film and television is Sun Jiazheng, the new vice-minister with specific responsibility for the film industry is Zhao Shi, and the new head of the Film Bureau is Liu Jianzhong. Their predecessors were not exactly purged (Tian Congming, the former vice-minister for film and a hardliner notorious for his earlier administration of Inner Mongolia and Tibet, retains a ministerial post), but the new brooms are clearly expected to sweep clean. They are there to do what their predecessors failed to do: to knock the film industry into economically viable shape. They themselves, however, are working under new constraints from the Propaganda Bureau.

Ding Guangen has consolidated his position as the loudest (hence, most influential) voice in the Propaganda Department with regular speeches calling for films to promote 'the lofty ideals, beliefs and excellent working system of the Communist Party...and nationalism' which are routinely printed in the 'intellectual daily' *Guangming Ribao*. Some studios have responded to his campaign by reverting to production of movies about 'model heroes'; the recent *Kong Fansen*, for example, celebrates the diligent and selfless career of the eponymous Party officer, who died in a road accident in 1994. But Ding convened a meeting in Changsha last April to discuss the whole question of film policy at which he made it plain that such films don't meet the needs of the moment. What are required, he explained, are *jinping* (literally, 'exquisite') films. Studio heads have been asking ever since what exactly this might mean, so far without clarification.

If no-one really knows what kind of film China 'should' be producing, then it's already clear enough what kinds of films the authorities can and cannot live with. The short list of foreign films acquired for legal distribution on a revenue-sharing basis in 1995 suggests what is acceptable these days: three Jackie Chan action-adventures from Hong Kong (*Rumble in the Bronx*, *Thunderbolt* and *Drunken Master II*) and a spot-sample of contemporary Hollywood escapism (*The Fugitive*, *Forrest Gump*, *Speed*, *The Lion King*). The 1996 list of approved imports includes *Toy Story*, *Babe*, *First Knight*, *Waterworld* and *Jumanji*. Disapproved titles include *Apollo 13* (too American-triumphalist and too embarrassing in the light of China's own space-race failures) and *GoldenEye* (too sexy, too violent). Needless to add, these and many hundreds of other titles unlikely to be passed for distribution in China already enjoy a wide 'underground' circulation on bootleg cassettes, pirated from Hong Kong, where they are routinely released with Chinese subtitles. It is not unknown for such tapes to be screened to paying audiences in state-owned mini-theatres in some regions of the country.

The Film Adminstration Regulations which came into force on 1 July limit the number of films that can be imported to 50 per annum, and the period these films can be screened to not more than one-third of the year in each cinema. Their sole concession to China's own film-makers is to make the Film Bureau less opaque in its decisions. The Bureau is now required to account for banning or demanding changes in films and for vetoing projects; its report must be in writing and delivered within 30 days of the film's submission. This will offer scant consolation to the many film-makers whose work is currently banned, blocked or stalled.

Zhang Yimou, for instance, submitted a script entitled *You Hua Haohao Shuo* (loosely: *Got a Problem? Talk about It!*) last spring, before the arrival of 'the new accountability'. He had the familiar experience of hearing nothing back from the Film Bureau but began production of the film regardless, assuming that approval would eventually be forthcoming. (The film is an urban comedy about a young intellectual who pursues his girlfriend when she leaves him for a richer man; it may have autobiographical resonances, given Zhang's break-up with Gong Li, but in no way courts political controversy.) The film wrapped in early August, but Zhang has *still* heard nothing from the Film Bureau. This puts him in the very awkward position of having made an 'illegal' film.

Chen Kaige's position, meanwhile, is more clear-cut. In May 1996, he was told that his *Temptress Moon* was banned in China; no reason given.

He submitted a new script in June; the Film Bureau turned it down in July, and Chen abandoned the project. He is now trying to come up with a new script. But Tian Zhuangzhuang, director of *The Blue Kite*, has given up all thought of directing films in the current political climate. De-blacklisted in 1995, he heads the quasi-autonomous production company Pegasé within Beijing Film Studio and is trying to help new directors make innovative features. But his first two productions are both stalled. *How Steel is Forged*, directed by Lu Xuechang, has been through two stages of censorship but remains unreleasable in the eyes of the Film Bureau. And *Girl from Vietnam*, directed by Wang Xiaoshuai (known for his 'illegal' feature *The Days*) has been shelved by the studio; studio head Han Sanping has evidently decided that he doesn't need the grief of explaining to the Film Bureau why he authorised a film about two crooks competing for the affection of a prostitute in Wuhan.

The only mainland director currently able to fulfil his promise is Zhang Yuan, who remains committed to unauthorised independent production; each of his films marks a concrete advance on the one before. He completed two films in 1996: the docu-drama *Sons*, in which a real-life dysfunctional family in Beijing re-enacts the episodes which led the alcoholic father to a mental hospital, and the entirely fictional *Behind the Forbidden City*, which explores the psychological implications of the sado-masochist relationship between a repressed, macho cop and a young gay man hauled in for overnight interrogation. Both films challenge longstanding taboos in China, but *Behind the Forbidden City* also opens a new chapter in Chinese culture. It offers not only the first open discussion of gay issues in modern China but also the first analysis of the bond between the state and its subjects in the metaphorical terms of sado-masochism.

Like everything Zhang has made since *Beijing Bastards* (1993), these films have been made and exported without any form of clearance from the Film Bureau. Zhang has been on a government blacklist since early 1994, but official disapproval seems to have had absolutely no effect on his ability to organise film productions or his freedom to travel. Some articles in the new Film Administration Regulations, however, target him in all but name. He is now threatened with arrest and imprisonment for producing unlicensed films if he persists in his 'crimes'. Many other film-makers, both inside and outside the 'system', are watching to see what happens to him. He previewed *Behind the Forbidden City* at the inaugural

Pusan Film Festival in South Korea last September, and plans to give it its official première in the Directors' Fortnight section at the 1997 Cannes Film Festival.

Threatened with arrest: Zhang Yuan (centre) filming Behind the Forbidden City *(1996)*

MOST HONG KONG films were, until recently, in profit before a single frame was shot. The territory's many producers were used to pre-selling their films in east and south-east Asia (and to overseas Chinese distributors worldwide) for more than it cost to make them. Taiwanese distributors alone could be expected to advance between two-thirds and three-quarters of the production costs of an average Hong Kong feature. This is no longer the case. Just as the Hong Kong domestic audience now prefers *Mission: Impossible* and *Independence Day* to most local movies, so the regional and overseas Chinese audience has dropped away sharply in the last two years. A producer is now lucky to get as much as one-sixth of his production cost from a pre-sale to Taiwan. The economic crisis has led some Hong Kong film-makers to look to California for backing for English-language movies. Several have followed John Woo's trail to Hollywood; the list already includes Kirk Wong, Ringo Lam and Tsui Hark, and others are certain to follow.

Journalists frequently try to link this exodus with China's impending resumption of sovereignty, but the attempt seems misguided. Freedom of expression has not been a live issue in Hong Kong cinema since 1982, the year in which Ann Hui released *Boat People*, a film about the North Vietnamese takeover of Danang widely read as a metaphor for Hong Kong's looming fate at the hands of China. That was also the year in which Tsui Hark's *Don't Play with Fire* and Patrick Tam's *Nomad* were banned in their original versions and sent back for rewriting and reshooting to make them 'acceptable' for Hong Kong release; both films offered deliberately provocative accounts of teenage delinquency. Since then, self-censorship has been as prevalent in the film industry as it is throughout the broadcast media and in most sectors of the press. No film-maker has wanted to commit career suicide by rocking the boat; the mixture of repressed anger and weary resignation with which the film community thinks about China matches society at large rather closely.

Insofar as Hong Kong film-makers have treated the space between Hong Kong and China, it has generally been with kid gloves. Yim Ho's drama *Homecoming* (1984) is typical: a woman worn down by the noise, pressure and urban grind of Hong Kong returns to her native village in Guangdong and rediscovers herself amid its rural tranquillity. Self-flagellation is a rare phenomenon in Hong Kong, but the premises underpinning Yim's storyline correspond with a romantic fantasy which seems be quite common; beyond its obvious meaning, this fantasy bespeaks a 'political' desire to think the best of China or to see it as positively as possible. Conversely, the several Hong Kong movies which have dealt with the issue of emigration and/or the quest for a third-country passport have avoided going into the *reasons* for emigrating, clearly bending over backwards to avoid exacerbating a difficult situation.

The one Hong Kong film which has countered this conspiracy of romanticisation and silence is Shu Kei's autobiographical documentary *Sunless Days* (1990), which goes into the lives and future options of the film-maker himself and his family and friends in the period immediately after the Tiananmen Square massacre of 1989. This film, by far the most engaged and moving response to the massacre by any Hong Kong artist, was financed by Japan's state broadcaster NHK and has never been seen on Hong Kong television. ❑

Tony Rayns *is a London-based film-maker, critic, lecturer and festival programmer*

LIU BINYAN

Trouble ahead

From his death bed, Deng Xiaoping looks out on a government that is the most corrupt and incompetent in China's history and a population that is more aware and more refractory than any before

DESPITE remorseless political repression since 1989, the Chinese regime has become steadily more anxious about political and social stability. Today's top leader, Jiang Zemin, confessed several months ago that he has felt 'terribly upset' and 'uneasy even when eating and sleeping'. A campaign to 'Strike Hard at Criminals' has been in full swing for over six months, and prisons all over the country are overflowing, but security remains an elusive goal. Control of the media has tightened and freedom of expression has been further suppressed. Nearly every dissident is now in prison or in exile. Politically, China has entered its darkest period since the advent of 'reform and opening' in 1979.

Today's China is a peculiar mix of Communist dictatorship and post-Communist society. The government has entirely lost its moral authority to rule and seems even to lack confidence in its own legitimacy. The people endure the regime only because of their fear that governmental collapse will bring social chaos. Whoever succeeds to power in the post-Deng era will face a truly daunting problem: while breathing life into the old Communist order seems virtually impossible, it seems no less difficult to forge a new order from today's confusion, whether by democratic means or strong-arm tactics.

Many Chinese have benefited from the economic reforms; a few privileged groups have profited immensely. But certain other, very large groups have not done so well. Agriculture grew rapidly in the early 1980s but since 1985 has stagnated. Faced with increasingly heavy and exploitative taxes, 130 million peasants have abandoned their fields to roam the country in search of better jobs. In the cities, economic reform has done nothing for 120 million workers in state-owned enterprises; on the contrary, it has severely undermined the security they once enjoyed. About half of these workers are now either unemployed or underpaid. In China's industrial cities, it is now common to see workers demonstrating in front of government offices to demand their salaries or relief funds. Deng Xiaoping's bargain with the Chinese people — roughly, 'You can make money provided you keep your mouths closed' — has recently become less and less effective, something that makes the regime more and more nervous. The possibility of workers' riots, which could lead to broader instability, hangs ominously over the country.

Store shelves are filled with goods but, except in the most wealthy areas, there are not many buyers. People feel uneasy about the future and are reluctant to spend their money. Twice in recent times the government has tried to stimulate consumption by reducing interest rates, but to little effect. People persist in trying to increase their incomes but opportunities are becoming harder and harder to find. Income disparities between rich and poor, between urban and rural areas, continue to grow.

Corruption has spread so thoroughly that it has become virtually synonymous with government itself. Corrupt officials and criminal gangs work hand-in-hand with each other. In many towns and villages, the gangs are in power — policing, settling disputes, extracting taxes — while the government acts as an official umbrella. The 'red' regime and the 'black' underworld are merging. Anti-corruption laws continue to be passed, but enforcement is entirely another matter.

The uneasy stability that survives in this inherently unstable situation results from widespread political cynicism and apathy among the populace. The people have no alternative political force to which they can turn; despite their anger, they feel so helpless and alienated they simply give up and do their best in the economic free-for-all.

Still, their repressed anger rankles. The Chinese people, who have been cruelly exploited, suppressed and deprived of their rights to participate in reforming their society, naturally feel that any revenge they might wreak, especially upon abusive and corrupt officials, is justified.

Today the most optimistic prospect for China, and perhaps the only way to avoid a disaster, is for people at the grass roots to take matters into their own hands. For years the Party prevented them from undertaking any spontaneous movements on their own, but there have recently been modest signs of change. In certain limited areas organisations have been able to survive provided they pose no threat to the leadership. Some

Subscribe!

United Kingdom & Overseas (excluding USA & Canada)

		UK:		Overseas:	
1 year (6 issues)			£38		£43
2 years (12 issues)			£66		£79
3 years (18 issues)			£96		£114

Name

Address

B7A1

£ _____ total. ❏ Cheque (£) ❏ Visa/MC ❏ Am Ex

Card No.

Expiry   Signature

❏ I would also like to send **INDEX** to a reader in the developing
world—just £25.

❏ I do not wish to receive mail from other companies.

INDEX, 33 Islington High St, London N1 9LH

Subscribe!

United States and Canada

	US:	
1 year (6 issues)		$50
2 years (12 issues)		$93
3 years (18 issues)		$131

Name

Address

B7B1

$ _____ total. ❏ Cheque ($) ❏ Visa/MC ❏ Am Ex

Card No.

Expiry   Signature

❏ I would also like to send **INDEX** to a reader in the developing
world—just $35.

❏ I do not wish to receive mail from other companies.

INDEX 33 Islington High St, London N1 9LH
Tel: 0171 278 2313 Fax: 0171 278 1878
Email: indexoncenso@gn.apc.org

INDEX ON CENSORSHIP
33 Islington High Street
London N1 9BR
United Kingdom

BUSINESS REPLY MAIL
FIRST CLASS PERMIT NO.7796 NEW YORK, NY

Postage will be paid by addressee.

INDEX ON CENSORSHIP
708 Third Avenue
8th Floor
New York, NY 10164-3005

officially-sponsored 'mass organisations' have begun to mobilise volunteers to promote public welfare at local levels. The village elections that went forward last year were an important step toward rural stability. When Deng Xiaoping dies, local leaders may take the opportunity to push through political reforms, and this may be the best hope for China.

But the rulers in Beijing, preoccupied with their power struggles, are moving in the opposite direction. The recent political clampdown in Beijing, combined with propaganda aimed at building a personality cult for Jiang Zemin, reminds people of the tense atmosphere on the eve of the Cultural Revolution in 1966. No-one knows what will happen but the fear of disaster creeps into people's minds. The voices of people cursing the regime can be heard everywhere, just as they could in the months before the protest movements of 1989. Small-scale disturbances have broken out, and have led local officials, especially in the south, to lose patience with the Jiang Zemin coterie in Beijing. Yet, even if a more enlightened reign replaced the Jiang regime overnight, it would still be enormously difficult for the centre to direct a revival in China.

China does not lack the spark to ignite a huge fire, but it does lack the torch that will lead it forward. One important reason for the failure of the 1989 Tiananmen movement was that the intellectuals were ill-prepared for such an opportunity: they had failed to educate the masses in the theory and strategy needed to lead the movement onto a rational course. Currently, some intellectuals claiming to be 'liberals', are being bought over by the regime. They become its spokespeople, enticing the people to compromise with the status quo. Others, though they endorse western democracy, think the ordinary people should be excluded from political participation. Except for western democracy and market economy, these intellectuals cannot present the people with an objective that tallies with the actual situation in China.

There is no force today that can frustrate the people's demand to change the current political and social order. But, since the Communist regime has blocked all legal and peaceful channels, they have no choice but to resort to violence. Unless society, with progressive elements within the Party, can halt the regime's march in the opposite direction and launch serious political reform, chaos in China is inevitable. ❏

Liu Binyan, a mainland journalist and writer, was expelled from the Communist Party in January 1988. He now lives in the USA and edits China Focus

SARAH SMITH

Protection racket

A SK anyone for advice on Chinese statistics and you get the same response: accurate information on China is 'limited' and 'always difficult to find'. This is partly a question of geography — the country's size and variety of social conditions render averages almost nonsensical. But it is largely a question of politics — China is hugely protective of what information it will give out and those statistics it does admit to are widely regarded as untrustworthy.

It is a country where estimates at a local level — such as the poverty line, which ranged in 1994 from 60 RMB a month in Xinjiang to 168 RMB in Shanghai — are more revealing than national averages. And where secrecy presents the researcher with an almost overwhelming problem: where to look and whom to trust. Nothing is available on the subject of sexual harassment (although it is reportedly widespread and increasing) or home ownership. The official verdicts on unemployment and HIV/AIDS are perceived by western commentators as presenting only the tip of the iceberg. The truth about male to female ratios can only be guessed at. A recent article in the Princeton-published *China Focus* even cast doubt on economic and industrial statistics. Only the revealing figures for film production buck the trend, suggesting as they do the impact more vigilant film censorship has had on the industry.

Sometimes the level of mendacity is breathtaking: *Chinese Statistical Yearbook* omits any reference to infant mortality in China, but is happy to provide figures for Taiwan and Hong Kong. What we can glean is often horrifying, for example, a female literacy rate of 62 per cent and infant mortality (according to the Chinese National working Committee for Women and Children) at 49.6 per 1,000 in central China and 85.4 per 1,000 in the west.

In contrast, Hong Kong is much more accessible and presents none of the shocks of Chinese statistics. But with one of the highest population densities in the world and a doctors per capita rating that is lower than China's, the former colony is not without problems. ❏

Sources: Economist Intelligence Unit, Europa - Far East & Australasia 1996, *British Foreign Office - North Asia & Pacific Research Analysts,* UNICEF, China Statistical Yearbook, China Labour Bulletin, China Focus, Far Eastern Economic Review, *WHO,* Hong Kong 1996, Hong Kong Annual Digest of Statistics 1995, *Hong Kong Institute of Human Resources Management, Hong Kong Information Services Department, Hong Kong Transition Project.*
Exchange rates: £1 = 13.396 RMB; US$1 = 8.3 RMB; US$1 = HK$ 7.736; £1 = HK$12.72

CHINA	HONG KONG
Area 9,571,300 sq km; **Population** 1.2 billion 1.3 billion by 2000; 28.62% urban, 71.38% rural, 51.02% male, 48.98% female, 55 minorities (6% of population) occupy 60% of country; Han (94%) occupy 40% **Population density** 90% of population inhabit little more than 15% of country, 2 per sq km Tibet; living space (rural) 20.2 sq m, (urban) 7.8 sq m **Birth rate** 17.70 per 1,000, **life expectancy** 69.4 (male 68, female 70.9), **infant mortality** (up to one year) 36.4 per 1,000 live births (urban 14.2, rural 41.6), **child mortality** (under 5 years) 43 per 1,000, **doctors** per 1,000 of population 1.57 **HIV/AIDS** ('love capitalism disease') officially estimated in 1995 as 3,341 cases HIV, 117 of AIDS, 82 deaths, (others estimate infection 50-100,000) **Official unemployment** 3.8%, World Bank estimate 10% in some urban areas, rising (by possibly half) by end of century to 268 million, women 44% of workforce, earn 149.6 RMB a month (77.45% of men's wages — 193.2 RMB a month), 25.1% of women workers earn less than 100 RMB a month (compared to 9.8% of men); 50% of secretaries working in joint venture companies have suffered **sexual harassment** **GDP** per capita $638 **Official poverty line** 530 RMB (cUS$100) **Literacy** 84% male, 62% female **Religion** Buddhist believers 100 million, Muslims 20 million, Christians 9 million **Films** 70 produced in 1996 (less than half made in 1995)	**Area** 1,084 sq km; **Population** 6.2 million, estimated rise in emigration 23% a year, 50.8% male, 49.2% female, 98% Chinese, 60% born in Hong Kong **Population density** HK island, Kowloon & New Kowloon 26,130 sq km, most dense Kwun Tong 53,610 sq km **Birth rate** 11.2 per 1,000, **life expectancy** 78.5 (male 75.7, female 81.3), **infant mortality** (up to 1) 5 per 1,000 live births, **child mortality** 6 per 1,000 (less than Germany), **doctors** 1.3 per 1,000 **HIV/AIDS** infection rates officially 642 cases HIV & 175 AIDS, (WHO estimate for 1994 3,000 cases of HIV) **Unemployment** 3.5%, women 38% of workforce, per capita net income (monthly) craftsmen and operatives HK$7,087 (US$916), white collar workers HK$10,153 (US$1312), 71.4% of workers think **sexual harrassment** a problem, 85.7% think equal opportunities exist **GDP** per capita HK$179,552 (US$23,200); after 1997 likely to account for 20% of China's national income; population of 6.2 million generate GDP equivalent to 18% of that produced by China's 1.2 billion **Religion** active Buddhists 650-700,000, Christians over 500,000, Muslims approximately 50,000, Hindus 12,000, Sikhs 3,000, Jews 1,000 503 **films** and videos made in 1995

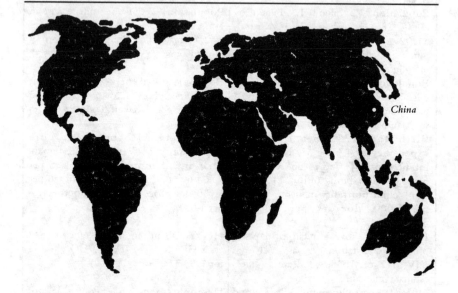

China

BARBARA VITAL-DURAND

Tea and no sympathy

The renewed repression of journalists in China has raised serious fears for the future of the media in Hong Kong. With the Chinese authorities blowing hot and cold over the new 'parameters of press freedom' the colony's return on 1 July 1997 is cause for alarm

HARSH measures are brought to bear on any form of 'dissident' expression in China, but particularly so on journalists and their contacts, who are kept under tight surveillance. As of 1 January last year, at least 14 journalists were in prison in China, of whom 12 have been there for several years: Yang Hong, Yu Dongyue and Sun Weibang (arrested in 1989); Chen Yanbin and Zhang Yafei (1990); Wu Shishen, Ma Tao and Liu Jingsheng (1992); Xi Yang, Samdrup Tsering, Tenpa Kelsang and Gao Yu (1993). Wei Jingsheng, arrested in 1979, was released briefly in 1993 but detained again in 1994 and sentenced to 14 years.

The arrests continued during 1996: Liu Xiaobo, literary critic and dissident, was arrested at his home on 8 October. Seven or eight police officers searched his house and seized a number of books and documents. The following day, Liu was sentenced by an administrative tribunal to three years of 're-education through labour'. His arrest was connected with the publication, several days before, of an open letter demanding, among other things, respect for freedom of expression. In March Hu Kesi, editor-in-chief of the magazine *Hong Kong Pacific Economy* and a veteran of the 1979 'Democracy Wall' movement, was arrested by state security agents and held incommunicado for several months. His current whereabouts are unknown.

China's relations with other countries — especially the USA — continue to determine the authorities' policy toward their opponents. On 6 November, a few days before a visit by US secretary of state Warren Christopher which Beijing described as 'crucial', Chen Ziming was granted a conditional release for medical reasons. However, he is forbidden to leave his apartment (other than to go to hospital under police escort) or to receive visits or take telephone calls. In mid-July, the doctors at Beijing's No 2 Prison, where he was being held in atrocious conditions, had diagnosed cancer of the right testicle and recommended immediate surgery. The authorities refused. His worsening state of health has led to fears for his life.

With the handover approaching, the Chinese authorities have not been slow in asserting their leading role on the Hong Kong political scene. The Hong Kong media, by issuing reassuring declarations and calls to adhere to the principles of 'Chinese-style journalism', are hoping to forestall any problems with their future masters. Journalists' organisations and free speech groups have been unsuccessful in getting the British authorities — or subsequently China's Preparatory Working Committee (PWC) — to abolish several legislative measures which, if left in place, will provide the Chinese authorities with some powerful weapons to use against the media (see page 132). Whether it is a matter of the regulations governing radio, television, public order or state secrets, the harsh experience of journalists on the mainland gives a clear hint of the difficulties that lie ahead. The increase in self-censorship is a good measure of how worried Hong Kong's journalists are.

On 14 February last year, the Chinese government forbade Hong Kong journalists from attending the PWC's first working session in Beijing. Also in February, the magazine *U-Beat*, produced by journalism students at the Chinese University of Hong Kong, told of pressures from the official Chinese news agency, Xinhua, to cut certain remarks a Chinese official had made in an interview. The journalists who did the interview were invited along for 'a cup of tea' and 'a moral lesson' about 'the respect due to high-ranking personalities during interviews, a lack of which would be extremely prejudicial to survival in the journalism profession'. On 3 May, China asserted its right to review applications for accreditation from journalists wishing to cover the handover ceremony. According to the *South China Morning Post*, the Chinese authorities demanded a right of 'joint appraisal' for every application.

If the Chinese authorities are reigning champions in the control of information — Internet users must register with the police within 30 days of opening an account so as not to 'harm' the country — other countries are competing hard. Singapore, which more than anywhere has linked its economic future to the explosion in multimedia technology, is in the first rank of Internet censors.

On 14 July, the authorities announced new measures for control of the Internet, completing a process begun in 1995. The Singapore Broadcasting Authority (SBA) ordered that the city-state's three Internet Service Providers (ISPs), all of which are owned by companies linked to the government, must block access to sites with 'questionable content'. The government has appointed a panel to come up with a definition of precisely what this constitutes. In addition, all political parties, ISPs, newspapers or private operators who maintain sites dealing with religion or politics were ordered to register with the SBA from 15 July. Any breach is punishable by a fine.

Meanwhile, state interference in the traditional media — radio, television, the press — continues as usual. ❏

Barbara Vital-Durand is the Asia-Pacific researcher for Reporters Sans Frontières, Paris

A censorship chronicle incorporating information from the American Association for the Advancement of Science Human Rights Action Network (AAASHRAN), Amnesty International (AI), Article 19 (A19), the BBC Monitoring Service Summary of World Broadcasts (SWB), the Committee to Protect Journalists (CPJ), the Canadian Committee to Protect Journalists (CCPJ), the Inter-American Press Association (IAPA), the International Federation of Journalists (IFJ/FIP), the International Federation of Newspaper Publishers (FIEJ), Human Rights Watch (HRW), the Media Institute of Southern Africa (MISA), International PEN (PEN), Open Media Research Institute (OMRI), Reporters Sans Frontières (RSF), the World Association of Community Broadcasters (AMARC), the World Organisation Against Torture (OMCT) and other sources

ALBANIA

On 18 October **Nusret Recica**, an ethnic Albanian from Kosovo was sentenced by a Tirana court to 10 months in prison for disseminating anti-constitutional writings. Recica pleaded guilty to distributing and trading various materials including writings by Enver Hoxha and other Communist leaders. He claimed he sold the books for financial reasons. (A19, Reuters, OMRI)

On 23 October the Appeal Court confirmed the prison sentences handed down to **Sami Meta, Timoshenko Pekmezi, Kristaq Mosko** and **Tare Isufi** for founding a Communist party (*Index* 3/1996, 6/1996). (SWB, AI)

The European Institute for the Media concluded on 28 October that there had been some improvement in media coverage of that month's elections in comparison with the past. The International Republican Institute also concluded that, despite some irregularities, no incidents seemed to threaten the elections' legitimacy. (European Institute for the Media, OMRI)

On 5 November the Appeal Court upheld prison sentences of up to 20 years that were given to nine high-ranking officials from the Communist era. The nine had been sentenced on 28 September for sending thousands of dissidents into internal exile. Shortly after the judgement a bomb exploded at the apartment of the chief judge in the case. (OMRI)

ALGERIA

Mokrane Hamoui, a journalist on the Arabic-language daily *Echourouk*, was murdered in Kouba, Algiers, on 13 October by a gang of men who attacked him in his car. The Islamic Armed Group claimed responsibility, justifying the murder on the grounds that the journalist was an apostate and the publication he worked for 'advocates vice and depravity'. (RSF, *Independent*)

Recent publication: *Fear and Silence — A Hidden Human Rights Crisis* (AI, November 1996, 45pp)

ARMENIA

The Yerevan city authorities withdrew permission for opposition rallies scheduled for 18 October, because of administrative errors in the application. The move followed President Ter-Petrosian's 11 October decree lifting the ban on public gatherings that was imposed after the unrest in the capital on 25 September (*Index* 6/1996). The opposition bloc National Accord (AHD) nevertheless held a rally in Yerevan on 25 October. An estimated 40,000 people participated. Vazgen Manoukian, the defeated presidential candidate, again charged that the 22 September election results were falsified and said the opposition will 'continue to struggle to replace the present government' through legal means. (OMRI)

AUSTRALIA

At the end of October Federal Parliament decided to ban photographs of the 1991 Dili massacre in East Timor from an exhibition about the island to be held at Parliament House because they were 'offensive'. The Australia East Timor Association described the ban as indicative of government policy towards East Timor, which has been one of 'censorship, repression and lack of free speech'. (*Sydney Morning Herald*)

Gregory Quincey, a computer studies student, was

acquitted in the Ipswich District Court in Queensland on 29 October of holding images of child pornography on his computer. He admitted to having downloaded the images, which he found at a Michigan University server, but claimed he had deleted them upon discovering what they were. Quincey's solicitor, Ian Dearden, said: 'If the prosecution had gone ahead, it would have said that curiosity on the Internet was a crime.' (*Sydney Morning Herald*)

Acting on a new censorship law passed on 1 November, Western Australia's state government says it will try to censor all computer transmissions of 'offensive' material. Computer games, Internet material, bulletin boards, e-mail, online computer services and regional and local computer networks will be censored. How this will be achieved has not yet been clarified. (Newsbytes News Network)

Federal government decided on 8 November to deny entry to both revisionist historian **David Irving**, and Sinn Fein leader **Gerry Adams**, as both men failed to meet the good character requirement under the Immigration Act. Civil liberties groups attacked the ban on Adams in particular, as a violation of free speech. John Howard said that Sinn Fein, was 'the political mouthpiece of a terrorist organisation', and that Adams' ban had 'precious little to do with free speech' (*Index* 6/1996). (*Times*, Reuters)

The High Court is currently reconsidering the 1994 **Theophanus** decision that there is an implied democratic right to freedom of speech on political matters in the Constitution (*Index* 6/1996). A decision is expected in March. (*Sydney Morning Herald*, Reuters)

Recent publication: *Too Many Open Questions — Stephen Wardle's Death in Police Custody* (AI, October 1996, 24pp)

AUSTRIA

The Klagenfurt offices of the Slovene-language magazine *Slovensky Vestnik* were broken into, ransacked and set on fire on 4 December, causing extensive damage which prevented the magazine from publishing. The attack came a week after *Slovensky Vestnik*, the weeklies *Nas Tednik* and *Nedelja* and the Slovene department of **Austrian Public Television** received threatening letters, decorated with swastikas, calling them 'Slovene pigs'. (RSF)

AZERBAIJAN

On 25 November censors ordered the newspaper *Azadlyg* to remove an article by Elchina Saldzhuga from the following day's edition. The piece was an analysis of recent changes in the government. On 26 November a cartoon appeared in place of the article, as censorship rules demand that the space left by censored articles must not be left blank. (*Ekspress-Khronika*)

Natella Bayramova, a jour-

nalist with the newspaper *Mukhalifat*, was forcibly deported from the Nakhichevan autonomous region to Baku on 1 December. Bayramova is well known for her articles on the human rights situation in Nakhichevan. (*Ekspress-Khronika*)

Azer Husseynbala, a journalist with *Azadlyg*, was stripped of his parliamentary accreditation on the order of the speaker, Murtuz Aleskerov, on 3 December, because of his satirical articles which 'negatively assessed the processes taking place in the republic'. Aleskerov said he would remove accreditation from any journalist who criticises Parliament or its members. (CPJ)

BELARUS

The independent station **Radio MBK** in Harodnia was ordered off the air on 8 October because of unspecified irregularities in its broadcasting contract. (SWB)

On 14 October President Lukashenka appointed Mikhail Shymanski as director-general and editor-in-chief of the parliamentary newspaper *Narodnaya Hazieta* in an attempt to convert the paper into a joint stock company and bring it under the control of the presidency. The Constitutional Court ruled the appointment invalid on 17 October. During the run-up to the referendum on the new constitution at the end of November, the paper continued supporting Parliament

SLAVAMIR ADAMOVICH

'A morsel of black bread'

On 25 November, the trial began of Slavamir Adamovich, the first poet in Belarus since the Stalinist era to be prosecuted for his writings. The poem in question, a satirical verse entitled 'Kill the President', appeared in the spring of 1995 in the Vitebsk independent paper *Vybar*. Adamovich was arrested a year later, in the aftermath of the Chernobyl memorial rally in Minsk, which was treated by the authorities as a subversive act and broken up violently by the police.

While in pre-trial detention, Adamovich went on hunger strike, which brought him close to death. He was taken into the intensive care unit of Minsk's KGB Hospital (the old name is still used), where he wrote the following poem:

A morsel of black bread,
Our own bread from our own rye,
Give to me, broken in two halves —
For you and for me — and moistened with honey
Still not solid, still fragrant with wax
And our wide spaces,
Let's have a snack my friend,
Let our bodies be replete
With the high energy of the primaeval forest
And the horizontals of the field.
After so many days of dying
There's a fragrance of the wild rain
In the mint and camomile posy
Brought us by an incognito
Woman from the newspaper *Name*.

KGB Hospital, 23 June 1996

Translated by Vera Rich

against the president. However, President Lukashenka signed a decree on 29 November dissolving the powers of the old Parliament, the day after signing his new version of the constitution into law. (SWB, *Ekspress-Khronika*)

On 14 November President Lukashenko announced his intention to expel Russian television journalists **Pavel Cheremet** of **ORT** and **Aleksandr Stoupnikov** of **NTV** for their 'lack of objectivity'. The announcement followed numerous verbal attacks made against the two by the president's supporters. Severe restrictions were placed on Russian broadcast media in the run-up to the referendum, including having e-mail links with Moscow cut off. (RSF, SWB)

BELGIUM

The Kurdish television station **MED TV** continues to suffer problems as a result of a police investigation (*Index* 6/1996), in the course of which betacam recorders, cables, archive material and highly sensitive footage filmed in Turkey were removed. This effectively closed down the production studios of the company. Although the authorities claim that this was not intentional and that MED TV is not itself under criminal investigation, the seized equipment has still not been returned. (IFJ)

BOSNIA-HERCEGOVINA

On 11 October **Michael Kirsch**, a freelance journalist and cameraman for Insight News Television (INTV), was assaulted by Bosnian Serb security forces while video-taping a destroyed house in Jusici, a Muslim village now inside Republika Srpska. IFOR retrieved and returned Kirsch's camera which had been confiscated, but the film was missing. Kirsch had reported that IFOR had filmed the attack and on 17 October a copy of the video was released to Kirsch and to INTV. (CPJ)

Zivko Savkovich, managing editor of the weekly independent newspaper *Alternativna* in Doboj, Republika Srpska, was given a one-month suspended sentence on 7

November for transmitting 'false material injurious to the honour and reputation of another'. The charge arose from an article published on 17 July 1996, claiming that officials of the Serbian Democratic Party (SDS) had blocked several opposition election meetings in Grabovica. Glas Srpski, the Banja Luka printing works refused to publish the 17th issue of *Alternativna* having already stopped printing two other independent papers, *Novi Prelom* and *Nezavisne Novine*. (CPJ, Institute for War and Peace Reporting, Alternativna Informativna Mreza)

On 13 November Bosnian Serb police closed down **Radio Krajina**, the Banja Luka station linked to General Ratko Mladic. The station, broadcasting since summer 1995, had been run by Mladic's former spokesman, Milovan Milutinovic and was critical of the Bosnian Serb ruling party. (OMRI, B&H Media Monitor)

Recent publication: *Monitoring the Media — The Bosnian Elections 1996* (IWPR and Media Plan, Sarajevo, November 1996, 18pp)

BRAZIL

On 20 October human rights lawyer **Francisco Gilson Nogueira de Carvalho** was shot dead on his doorstep in Natal, Rio Grande do Norte. He was killed by 13 bullets, most of them to the head. Carvalho was known for his work investigating civil

police involvement in the activities of the death squad Meninos de Ouro (Golden Boys), who are thought to be responsible for numerous killings, cases of torture and death threats mostly carried out in the poor neighbourhoods of Natal. There is now concern for the safety of Robert Monte and Luiz Gonzaga Dantas, two of Carvalho's colleagues at the Centre for Human Rights and Collective Memory, after their names were discovered on a death list. All three men had received federal police protection in mid-1995 following regular death threats, but this was withdrawn after six weeks. (AI)

Recent publication: *Human Rights Violations and the Health Professions* (AI, October 1996, 20pp)

BULGARIA

On 14 November the Constitutional Court overturned 15 provisions of the **Radio and Television Act**, including the establishment of a National Broadcasting Council with the right to approve programme schedules and content and to cancel programmes. Also declared unconstitutional were articles depriving the judiciary of free airtime and banning journalists from giving 'subjective' commentaries. President Zhelev had tried to veto the law in August (*Index* 5/1996, 6/1996). (OMRI)

Recent publication: *Bulgarian Authorities Respond to Amnesty International's June 1996*

Report (AI, October 1996, 7pp)

BURMA

U Kyi Maung (*Index* 4/1995), member of the opposition NLD's Central Executive Committee, was detained by the security forces in the early hours of the morning of 23 October, on suspicion of encouraging student unrest at Yangon Institute of Technology, Rangoon. Some 100 students are believed to have been detained during the course of a three-day protest, which was broken up by armed police. U Kyi Maung was released on 28 October. (HRW, *Guardian*)

NLD leader **Aung San Suu Kyi** faced intimidation and continued disruption to her weekly meetings throughout October and November. On 3 November police briefly detained at least four of her supporters and barred vehicles and pedestrians from her home. Suu Kyi herself was attacked on 9 November when stones were thrown at cars in her motorcade by a group of young men, believed to have been brought in by the government from neighbouring towns. Further road blockades were set up on 16 November, preventing the planned visit of a representative of the World Council of Churches to Suu Kyi's home, and on 23 November. The latter block was defied by Suu Kyi who managed to speak for five minutes to supporters a kilometre away before riot police arrived to disperse

them. (Reuters, SWB)

A student protest, which began with a sit-in at the Yangon Institute of Technology on 2 December and then moved on to the streets of central Rangoon, was brought to a close by armed police in the early hours of 3 December. More than 600 students were briefly detained after they refused a police order to disperse after one of the biggest street protests since the 1988 pro-democracy uprisings. Access to Aung San Suu Kyi's home was again blocked off for several days in order to prevent protesters rallying outside. Further student protests between 6 and 10 December were broken up by riot police with water cannon. (*Guardian*, *Telegraph*, Reuters, SWB)

CAMEROON

Pius Njawe, editor-in-chief of *Le Messager Popoli*, was arrested at the paper's offices on 29 October following his sentencing earlier in the month (*Index* 6/1996). He was held until his release on bail on 15 November. His colleague **Eyoum Ngangue**, sentenced to a year's imprisonment, has not been arrested. (World Press Freedom Committee, RSF, AI)

Evariste Menouga, a reporter for the paper *Le Nouvel Indépendant*, was detained in Yaounde on 27 November and questioned about his work and about another journalist with the paper, Peter William Mandio. Mandio was also arrested

around 7 December, apparently in connection with an article criticising the minister of public works. Meanwhile, **Daniel Atangana**, a journalist with the weekly *Le Front Indépendant*, was arrested on 10 December after writing an article about the commander of the presidential guard. And the weekly *La Nouvelle Expression* has been banned for 'disturbing public order' in an article implicating the deputy interior minister in the poor management of a commercial bank. (RSF, AI)

CANADA

In October federal laws limiting electoral campaign expenditure were overturned. The **Canada Elections Act** prevented private citizens from spending more than US$800, independently of a political party during an election campaign in the promotion or opposition of a party or candidate. Infringements were punishable by up to five years in prison. (*Financial Post*)

The Canadian Radio, Television and Telecommunications Commission has placed restrictions on the use of fax advertising, permitting 'junk' faxes only from 9am to 9.30pm Monday to Friday, and 10am to 6pm on weekends. (Reuters)

The House of Commons Health Committee recommended a phased introduction of new restrictions on tobacco advertising on 12 December. The new rules would ban all broadcast, billboard, street-kiosk, bus-panel and counter-top display advertisements, vending machines, and the use of company logos on non-tobacco products. Print advertising, and event sponsorship would be severely curtailed. Tobacco companies call the measures 'extreme and ineffective and likely illegal'. (Reuters, *Financial Post*)

CENTRAL AFRICAN REPUBLIC

Marcel Mokwapi, managing editor of the daily *Le Novateur* (*Index* 6/1996), was placed in preventive custody on 24 October. A one-year jail term was requested by the federal public prosecutor. Mokwapi's conviction stemmed from charges filed by judge Alain Gbaziale who claimed he was defamed by two articles in June and August 1996. (RSF)

CHILE

The authorities barred all public demonstrations from areas near the Ibero-American summit from 9-11 November, frustrating anticipated protests against the visit of Cuba's President Castro. The Interior Ministry said that any foreigners found to be involved in actions disrupting public order and domestic security would be expelled from the country. (Reuters, *El Mercurio*)

On 31 October the Supreme Court of Justice rejected a petition brought by the military prosecutor to close legal proceedings in all cases of human rights violations committed before March 1978, during the military government. In a majority vote of

14 to one, the Court reasserted the independence of the judiciary by stating that 'judges have independence to decide...on cases within their jurisdiction. In this regard, any external influences, from sources other than the judiciary, and internal influences from higher authorities... are inadmissible.' (AI)

CHINA

Following a 17-month period of detention, dissident **Wang Dan** was formally charged on 7 October with conspiring to overthrow the government. He was found guilty after a four-hour closed trial on 30 October, sentenced to 11 years' imprisonment and stripped of his political rights for a further two years. Foreign journalists were banned from the court and two foreign camera crews in the vicinity had their film confiscated. The only reference to the trial in the Chinese media came in an English-language daily. (*Guardian*, *Independent*, HRW)

On 11 October controversial novelist and screenwriter **Wang Shuo** revealed that his publishing house has been ordered to stop printing editions of his best-selling four-volume collected works. His publisher, the state-owned Hua Yi, has been forced to write a self-criticism for publishing 'vulgar and reactionary' works. Wang's screenplay *Papa* has also been banned. (Reuters, *International Herald Tribune*)

Activist **Wang Xizhe** (*Index*

4/1996, 6/1996) fled China on 12 October, arriving in America on 15 October, six days after dissident and critic **Liu Xiaobo** was sentenced to three years' 're-education through labour' for a statement they jointly issued on 30 September (see page 110). (Reuters, *International Herald Tribune*)

China moved against writers, journalists, and their newspapers in a wave of repression following the Sixth Plenary Session of the Communist Party Central Committee in October. First, dozens of publications within the state banking system were ordered to close in late October under a new regime of 'macro-level controls and adjustments'. Other victims included the Shenzen magazine *Focus* and Beijing's *Orient*, both of which were suspended after publishing proscribed material. In early November Shanxi party official Liu Ronghui took up the Sixth Plenary Session's theme and called on writers to avoid negative western influences, uphold 'Marxist realism', and focus on China's reform and modernisation. A week later the state ideological departments announced a quota for the closure of one third of China's 3,600-plus provincial and municipal newspapers and periodicals, as well as any internal publications that had not been officially registered, to be met by 1 March 1997. In addition, the State Council has demanded that all newspapers and periodicals, radio and television stations, dance halls and places of public entertainment pay the government a 3 per cent 'cultural undertaking fee' by January 1997. This could force small publications under financial strain to close. (*Nikkei Weekly*, SWB, Reuters, *China Focus*)

Hong Kong democracy activists **Wong Chung-ki** and **Chui Pak-tai** were expelled from China on 1 November for 'disrupting public order' by calling a press conference and distributing material at a Beijing hotel. The pair had travelled to the mainland to protest the method of selection for the government of the colony after June 1997. (*South China Morning Post, Independent*)

Chen Ziming (*Index* 3/1994, 4/1995) was released from his 13-year prison sentence on 6 November. Chen, who is suffering from cancer, was released on medical parole in 1994 but arrested again in 1995 after he supported dissident petitions on the anniversary of the Tiananmen massacre. (*International Herald Tribune*)

On 26 November pro-democracy activists **Shen Liangqing, Ma Lianggang** and **Huang Xiuming** stood trial in Hefei, Anhui province, on charges of spreading counter-revolutionary propaganda and incitement stemming from three articles written and distributed in 1991. They had already been detained for a year. (Reuters)

The Ministry of Culture announced on 12 December that it had banned imports of

all art or artistic activites that have 'the goal of splitting China and its nationalities'. (Reuters)

COLOMBIA

Josué Giraldo Cardona, president of the Meta Civic Human Rights Committee (CCDHM) and an activist with the Patriotic Union (UP), was shot dead outside his home on 13 October. His killing renews fears for the safety of other CCDHM members who, like Giraldo, have received death threats. Three days before his killing, **Rafael Gonzales Barraza**, secretary-general of the Workers' Trade Union (USO), was killed by two gunmen in the El Cerro district of Barrancabermeja, department of Santander. (AI)

Norvey Díaz, director of the programme *Rondando por los Barrios* on Radio Colina, was murdered in the resort town of Girardot on 18 October. His body was found with a single bullet wound in the nape of the neck. Investigators believe that his murder was carried out by professional hitmen. Díaz had reported on the alleged involvement of police officials in the murder of street dwellers, as well as on corruption and the drug trade. (RSF)

On 20 October **Manuel Vincente Pena Gómez**, a journalist for the popular daily *La Prensa de Bogotá*, was ambushed by several gunmen who opened fire on his car with automatic weapons. He was protected

from injury by his armoured car. (RSF)

CONGO

Ben Ossete Obelas, director of the independent monthly *Le Choc*, was sentenced to eight months in prison for 'spreading false news and defamation'. The sentence was handed down after publication in the magazine's 1-15 October edition of an article accusing the management of the National Security Office of embezzlement. (RSF)

CROATIA

On 13 October journalists announced plans to set up an independent television network. The move followed the cancellation of a popular late-night show on state television (HRT) featuring foreign news coverage of Croatia. The new channel, named **TV Network**, opened on 1 December. (SWB)

On 20 November **Radio 101**, the last independent radio station in Croatia, was refused a licence by the Croatian Telecommunications Council on the grounds that it is 'not objective'. Widespread protests followed, including a gathering of about 6,000 people and letters of support from state news agencies. Radio Globus, having been offered the frequency instead, announced that it would reject it. (RSF, CPJ, AMARC, *Independent*)

On 26 November **Vesna Jankovic**, editor-in-chief, **Dejan Krsic**, executive editor

LIU XIAOBO & WANG XIXHE

The nationality question

On 10 October last year, the anniversary of China's National Day marking the 1911 revolution, the Hong Kong newspaper Ming Pao *carried the text of a declaration addressed by the leading Chinese dissidents Liu Xiaobo (now serving 11 years in a re-education through labour camp) and Wang Xizhe (now in exile in the USA) to both the Chinese Communist Party and to the Kuomintang (KMT) of Taiwan.*

Liu and Wang contended that, although the Chinese Communist government was the sole legitimate ruler of all China, it had reneged on many of the rights given to citizens in early versions of the constitution and on promises held out to minority peoples about self-rule. They supported their arguments with chapter and verse from the constitution and other founding documents of the Chinese Communist Party (CCP).

They also called for the impeachment of President Jiang Zemin for claiming that the People's Liberation Army was answerable only to the CCP rather than to the National People's Congress as stipulated in the constitution.

Xixhe and Liu argued further that contrary to the sentiment among other Chinese people, as in Taiwan, Hong Kong and throughout the east Asian diaspora, China's reluctance to pursue its claim to the Diaoyu Islands — ownership of which is disputed with Japan — demonstrated that the Party is practising what it accused the Kuomintang of doing in the 1940s, namely appeasing Japanese militarism.

The Tibet issue

'Throughout the world today, the right of national self-determination is a basic human right. It is not only contained in the first article of the UN Convention on Human Rights and generally recognised by the international community, it is also a basic principle advocated by Marxism-Leninism.

During the revolutionary war years, the CCP vigorously advocated the right of national self-determination. In the Constitutional Programme of the Chinese Soviet Republic set up in Ruijin, Jiangxi, the CCP not only acknowledged the right of ethnic minorities in China to self-determination, but boldly announced it 'will consistently acknowledge that various weak minority nationalities have

and **Veronika Reskovic** of the magazine *Arkzin* were summoned for questioning by the police in connection with an article published on 13 September under the pseudonym Bozo Matic, which cited an estimate made in a foreign newspaper of President Tudjman's personal wealth. (*Arkzin*)

CUBA

Bernardo Arevalo Padron, correspondent for the Puerto Rican-based agency **Free and Independent Press for Cuba** (PPLIC), was detained by eight State Security agents in Vertientes, Camagüey province on 17 October. Arevalo was taken to State Security headquarters in Camagüey, where he was held in a windowless cell and told that, as a correspondent the right to break away from China to set up independent states'.

Mao Zedong, chairman of the Soviet Republic, also specifically announced in his policy address that 'the Mongol, Hui, Tibetan, Miao, Li and Gaoli peoples can voluntarily decide whether to break away from the Soviet Federation [as published] to set up independent regions'.

In the Ten Programmes for Resisting Japanese Aggression and Saving the Country, the right of national self-determination remained the CCP's policy.

In his report to the Seventh CCP National Congress, Mao Zedong cited Sun Yat Sen's declaration while commenting on the nationality policies of the future coalition government advocated by the CCP. He said:

'In 1924, in his Declaration of the First KMT National Congress, Sun Yat Sen said... the KMT solemnly announces it acknowledges the right of self-determination of the various nationalities within China. They should set up a free and unified republic of China (a coalition jointly set up by the various nationalities of their own free will) after winning victory in opposing imperialism and the revolution against the warlords.'

Mao Zedong added: 'The CCP fully agrees with Mr Sun's nationality policy.'

Wang Xizhe and Liu Xiaobo also fully support this liberal and progressive policy of Mr Sun and the CCP.

However, after seizing political power, the CCP once again failed to honour its promise. On 5 October 1949, less than one year from the founding of the People's Republic of China, the CCP Central Committee issued a document containing criticisms and instructions to the Front Committee of Deng Xiaoping's second field army, then on its way to southwest China, an area inhabited by ethnic minorities:

'It is necessary not to stress the right of national self-determination for ethnic minorities. During the civil war, to win over minority nationalities in our opposition the KMT's reactionary rule (the KMT displayed notable Han chauvinism before the ethnic minorities), our party stressed the slogan. This was absolutely right.'

From Ming Pao, *Hong Kong, in Chinese, 10 October 1996*

© *BBC Worldwide Monitoring, Summary of World Broadcasts*

for a foreign news agency, he was under the influence of enemy propaganda. He was released after five days and given 24 hours to leave Camagüey. (RSF)

María de los Angeles González, Havana corre-spondant for PPLIC, was questioned by police on 24 October over information she sent to correspondents in the USA. Her home is currently under surveillance. (RSF)

On 29 October **Gustavo Rodríguez Delgado** and **José García Díaz**, reporters for the news agency **Centro Norte del Pais** (CNP), were arrested by police and taken to the State Security prison in Santa Clara. They were questioned about their jobs and threatened with 16-year prison terms if they continued their work as journalists. They were released the next day. (RSF)

ECUADOR

President Abdala Bucaram singled out the Quito daily *Hoy* for criticism in early December, saying that it had fostered 'regionalist' prejudices, particularly between the cities of Quito and Guayaquil. Television ads were also aired in which an anonymous announcer told people not to read *Hoy* but rather to 'believe in the future of the national government'. (IAPA)

EGYPT

The 20-26 October edition of the English-language weekly *Middle East Times* was banned from distribution by the information minister because the front page contained a reference to an article about President Mubarak's 15 years in power, which had been scheduled to run inside the paper but which had been removed by the censors. The article, by staff writer **Steve Negus**, accused Mubarak of creating a cult of personality and alleged that Egypt had more political prisoners than at any time in its history. The Arabic weekly *al-Dustour* was also banned. No reason was given but the ban came 10 days after Israel complained to the Egyptian foreign minister, Amr Moussa, about a picture of Israel's prime minister with a swastika on his forehead. The censors' office claimed that they had the right to restrict newspapers

which are licensed abroad. *Al-Dustour* is licensed in Cyprus, *Middle East Times* in Greece. In August the Cyprus-based Arabic monthly *al-Tadamun* was banned for suggesting that Arab leaders undergo mental tests. (RSF, *Middle East Times*)

Two academics at the University of Cairo — agricultural engineer **Mahmoud Ahmad al-Areeny** and economics and politics lecturer **Abd al-Hamid al-Ghazali** — were sentenced to three years in prison in November after being found guilty of membership of the banned **Muslim Brotherhood**. Their conviction may also be connected to their involvement in a new Islamist party, al-Wasat. (AAASHRAN)

Parliament agreed on 7 December to increase the penalties against 'unauthorised' mosque preachers to over E£100 (US$29) or a month in jail, or both, in order to halt the spread of 'deviant' ideas. In October the government announced that it intended to take control of 30,000 private mosques — the favoured platform for radical Islamists — and appoint graduates from state-run al-Azhar Islamic university to run them under the auspices of the Ministry of Religious Endowments. (Reuters)

EL SALVADOR

On 8 October two unidentified men attempted to kidnap **Eliezar Ambelis**, an activist with the **Madeleine Lagadec Human Rights Centre**. An

hour later his colleagues received a threatening phone call at the Centre's San Salvador office and in the evening, a written death threat was left outside the office in Santa Clara. On 12 October the Centre's offices in Santa Ana were broken into and office equipment and documents taken. The threats are thought to be related to the work of the Centre in promoting voting rights and in campaigning against the death penalty. (AI)

On 17 October **Ricardo Tobar**, a cameraman with the privately-owned television station Canal 12, was beaten and tear-gassed by a National Civilian Police (PNC) officer during a demonstration by war veterans in San Salvador. Tobar was covering clashes between police and demonstrators who were moving to occupy Congress. (AI)

ETHIOPIA

Taye Belachew, editor-in-chief of the independent magazine *Tobia*, was arrested without charge on 22 November. Three days later the magazine's deputy editor, **Anteneh Merid**, was also arrested. They were interrogated by police about an article in the November issue, entitled 'A Strategy to Reunite Eritrea with Ethiopia'. **Goshu Moges**, acting manager of the company which publishes *Tobia*, was also arrested without charge on 12 December. The previous day, **Akilu Tadesse**, editor-in-chief of the weekly *Ma'ebel*, was arrested without charge. (CPJ)

Recent publications: *Imprisonment and Denial of Justice* (RSF, October 1996, 20pp); *The Human Rights Situation* (Ethiopian Human Rights Council, September 1996, 13pp)

FRANCE

Two rap musicians were jailed for three months and banned from performing for six months in mid-November for 'insulting behaviour towards people in authority during the exercise of their duties, by making injurious remarks before a public of several thousand people'. The prosecution against **Bruno Lopez**, alias Kool Shen, and **Didier Morville**, alias Joey Star, of the group **NTM**, was brought by 26 police officers who were on crowd duty at a concert at La-Seyne-sur-mer on 14 July 1995, held to protest the election of the town's National Front mayor. (*Times*)

On the evening of 1 December the Upper Corsica offices of the daily *La Corse* were damaged by a small bomb explosion, with three people suffering minor injuries from flying glass. The windows of the daily *Corse-Matin*, located opposite, were also destroyed. No-one has claimed responsibility for the attack, which is similar to attacks on *Corse-Matin* in 1992 and 1994. (RSF)

Under rules governing the distribution of foreign publications, the 17 October issue of the Algerian daily *Liberté* was seized by the French air and border police. No official reason was given, but the seizure was thought to be associated with an article commemorating the 35th anniversary of a demonstration of Algerians in Paris that was violently suppressed by French security forces. The article, entitled 'When the Seine Rolled with Corpses', refuted the official statistics which state that three died and 64 were injured. There are thought to have been 200 deaths. (RSF)

GERMANY

Simon Wiesenthal, the veteran Nazi-hunter, has criticised plans to close the **Central Agency**, Germany's main body for investigating crimes committed during the Nazi regime. Some of Germany's 16 states want the storage of hundreds of thousands of files and 1.5 million index cards moved to the federal archives as a cost-cutting measure. Wiesenthal said of the agency: 'No institution has done more for the honour of Germany than the Central Agency in Ludwigsburg.' Willi Dressen, director of the agency, expressed concern that many of the files it held would fall apart, and endanger the task of reminding younger Germans about the Third Reich. (*Times*)

GHANA

Opiesie Nkansaa-Daaduam, a columnist with the weekly *Free Press*, was arrested on 25 November and taken to the Bureau of National Investigation by military police for questioning about a 'subversive and treasonable article'. In the article, published on 20 November, he accused President Rawlings of vote-rigging and a military officer of planning a coup. (RSF, PEN)

GREECE

In September the Post Office refused to allow *Moglena*, the publication of the Human Rights Movement of the Macedonians in Greece, to be mailed at the cheaper rate available to officially registered publications. Representatives of *Moglena* and of *Zora*, a Rainbow Party publication, were summoned by the police on 9 October as part of an investigation into the content of the publications. (Greek Helsinki Monitor)

Recent publication: *Unfair Trials of People Arrested at Athens Polytechnic University* (AI, October 1996, 27pp)

GUATEMALA

Ortiz Morales, one of the founders of the Co-ordinating Committee for the Mayan Peoples' Organisations in Guatemala (COP-NAGUA), disappeared on 5 October in Escuintla. He was found dead a week later. His body showed signs of torture. Student unionist **Hector Tavico Laguarca** was also found dead several days after disappearing on 31 October. Several students from the School of Anthropology and History Association have also received threats and intimidation. (OMCT, CODEHU-CA)

Israel Hernández Marroquín, a journalist with the weekly *Infopress Centroamericano* and a university professor, was murdered in Guatemala City on 11 December. The motives for the killing are unclear. (FIP)

GUINEA-BISSAU

José Rodríguez Santy, director of the radio station **Pigiguitty**, alleged on 9 October that threats had been made against one of his journalists by members of the Cabinet of prime minister Saturnino Da Costa. The ministers allegedly met the father of newscaster **Ladislau Stanislau Robalo** and told him to pressure his son to stop spreading 'lies' on the air. Otherwise, they said, he would be taken to a police station and beaten so badly 'his father would not even recognise him'. (RSF)

HONDURAS

On 8 October **Jorge Luis Monroy**, a local commentator for the daily radio programme *Las Verdades del Aire* in Octopeque, was assaulted by two men who broke into the studio during transmission of the programme. Monroy was threatened with death if he continued to broadcast or reported the attack. The men have been identified but no charges have been brought against them. (CPJ)

On 3 November *La Tribuna* journalists **Enma Evangelina Calderón Umanzor** and **Julio Cesar Antúnez** were assaulted by Jimmy Macoto,

the husband of the executive director of the National Institute of Retirement Pensions for Public Employees. As Antúnez was taking photos of the couple's vehicle, Macoto insulted the journalists and threatened them with a gun. The journalists believe that the incident stems from an article in the 26 December 1995 edition of *La Tribuna* which reported that Oqueli de Macoto had been seen driving a brand-new sports car. (IAPA)

HONG KONG

In October China revealed new regulations governing control of society and the media in Hong Kong. Under the new ordinance international anti-Communist and anti-China organisations are banned from the colony, anti-China activities, such as the annual Tiananmen Massacre demonstrations, are prohibited, and Taiwanese institutions are forbidden to organise events advocating 'two Chinas'. The island is not to act as a refuge or transfer station for hostile elements or criminals from China. Strictures covering the media include a ban on the dissemination of colonial and western ideology, references to 'Taiwan's independence' or 'self-determination for Hong Kong', and slander of the mainland government. (*China Focus*)

In late November the British Hong Kong government announced its intention to introduce legislation defining treason, sedition, subversion,

and secession in preparation for China's takeover of the colony in 1997. The move was criticised by the Chinese Foreign Ministry as 'meddling in the affairs of the Hong Kong Special Administrative Region'. (Reuters)

INDIA

The Marathi tabloid *Aaj Dinank* was closed down on 16 October after pressure from the Shiv Sena in Maharashtra. The paper's editor, Kapil Patil, had been highly critical of Shiv Sena in his editorials, especially with regard to a controversial murder case in which he alleged Shiv Sena had played a part. (*Hindu*)

Newspaper and television journalists were beaten outside the Delhi home of Bahujan Samaj Party leader Kanshi Ram on 25 October. The reporters were covering a political meeting at Ram's house and were attacked without provocation. An official complaint brought against Ram has not been followed up. A protest march by journalists the following day was broken up by police using tear gas. (*Frontline*)

Two photographers with the daily *Mathrubhumi* in Kerala, **C Sunil Kumar** and **Santhosh G Krishnan**, reported being beaten by youth wing activists of the ruling Communist Party of India (Marxist) on 28 October at Kottayam. They were trying to take photographs of students who have been accused in a political murder case. (*Mathrubhumi*)

The Miss World beauty contest held at the end of November in Bangalore provoked widespread protests by Hindu and feminist groups. African contestants, meanwhile, accused the Indian media of racism, saying they were being ignored because of their colour. One man burned himself to death in protest and the police rounded up dozens of suspected troublemakers. An attempt to have the pageant banned by a court order failed when the court ruled that the contest could go ahead provided there was no indecent exposure, obscenity or nudity. (*Times*)

Recent publication: *Police Abuse and Killing of Street Children* (HRW, November 1996, 189pp)

INDONESIA

After a series of verbal and written warnings the officially sanctioned Indonesian Journalists' Association (PWI), withdrew its approval from **Emran Goesti**, editor-in-chief of weekly news magazine *D&R* on 16 October. Goesti has been accused of allowing members of the unofficial Alliance of Independent Journalists (AJI) to work on the magazine. Officially, publications can only be produced under a PWI-approved editor and *D&R* has been told to appoint a new editor-in-chief within three months. Staff at the tabloid *Kontan* have also recently come under pressure

to revoke its staff's AJI membership. (Institute for Study of the Free Flow of Information, RSF)

In mid-October President Suharto moved to ban mass outdoor campaign rallies, the only available forum for political demonstrations in Indonesia. The rallies, which are only permitted for four weeks before an election, will be replaced by indoor discussions. Observers believe the president's reforms are aimed at shoring up the chances of the ruling party, Golkar, in the May elections. (*Guardian*)

On 28 October police raided the printing house of leading underground newspaper *Suara Independen* in south Jakarta, arresting manager **Andi Syahputera** and operator **Nasrul** and confiscating 5,000 copies of the October issue. Both men have been charged with distributing printed material defaming President Suharto and liable to disturb stability. *Suara Independen* is published by the Melbourne-based Society of Indonesian Alternative Media which specialies in publishing uncensored news not found in the mainstream media. (RSF, Institute for Study of the Free Flow of Information)

On 1 November the government announced plans to crack down on 32 NGOs which it regards as 'problematic' and to bring all Indonesia's 8,000 NGOs into line with the 1985 laws governing mass organisations. Those under attack, including the Indonesian Legal Aid

Foundation and the Indonesian Labour Welfare Union, stand accused of failing to specify the state ideology, Pancasila, as their philosophy and conducting illegal activities. Under the 1985 ruling all NGOs must obtain government approval and report any foreign financial support they receive. The move is believed to be aimed at new political groups, such as the New Masyumo Muslim organisation, whose names recall banned political groups of the past. (Reuters, *South China Morning Post*, *Jakarta Post*)

A book on the ousted Democracy Party of Indonesia (PDI) leader, **Megawati Soekarnoputri**, came under investigation by the public prosecutor in early November. The book, *Never Retreat*, has been published by the Institute for the Study of the Free Flow of Information. (*Asia Intelligence Wire*)

Twenty foreign correspondents had their newly issued visas for travel to East Timor unexpectedly cancelled on 21 November. No reason was given. (RSF)

All 124 of opposition leader Megawati's supporters detained during the Jakarta riots in July (*Index* 5/1996) were released from jail on 28 November, following their trial for refusing to obey police orders. Nine were acquitted and the remaining 115 sentenced to approximately four months in jail, time they had already served in custody. The more serious charges of assault were all dropped. (*Sydney Morning Herald, Guardian*)

IRAN

On 2 November, **Heshmatollah Tabarzadi**, editor of the radical Islamic weekly *Payam-e-Daneshjoue*, was arrested and imprisoned following a complaint from the Ministry of Islamic and Cultural Guidance, that he had resumed publishing his banned magazine without permission (*Index* 4/1996). He was released on bail on 9 November. (Reuters)

Faraj Sarkoohi, editor of the independent literary magazine *Adineh*, disappeared on 3 November after going to Tehran airport to board a flight to Germany, where he was due to meet his wife. The official Iranian newspaper *Jomhouri-e-Eslami* claimed on 13 November that Sarkoohi had boarded the plane and that he disappeared after arrival in Germany. Sarkoohi's colleagues, however, believe that he is being held secretly in Iran. (Iranian PEN Centre in Exile, RSF)

On 11 November, the body of the writer **Ghaffar Hosseini** was found in his apartment. The authorities claim that Hosseini died of a heart attack. However, colleagues report that he had no history of heart trouble or disease. Like Faraj Sarkoohi, Hosseini was a signatory to the 1994 declaration of 134 Iranian writers, calling for an end to literary censorship (*Index* 6/1994). (Iranian PEN Centre in Exile)

IRELAND

Suspicions of police collaboration with the crime boss who ordered the killing of investigative journalist **Veronica Guerin** have come to light as the investigation into her murder has progressed (*Index* 4/1996). At least 15 police officers have been caught up in the investigation, which has implicated officers as sources of information about Guerin's movements passed on in turn by a suspec. A senior Dublin politician stated off the record that information had come to light 'mainly involving claims that Gardai were consorting with, or in the pay of, criminals'. (*Independent*)

ISRAEL

A religious party, Shas, whose support in the Knesset the Likud government depends on for its majority, has threatened to withdraw that support unless **Gil Kopatch**, a satirist of biblical stories on a weekly spot on State TV's *Week's End* show, is banned. Kopatch has referred to Eve as the world's 'first sex bomb' and Noah as an alcoholic 'with his willy out'. Shas accuse him of treating the Bible with contempt. (*Irish Times*)

Recent publication: *Journalists in the Line of Fire* (RSF, November 1996)

JAPAN

The full text of **DH Lawrence's** *Lady Chatterley's Lover* was published in translation by Shinchosha publish-

ing house on 30 November. The new edition includes passages still officially banned under a 1950 ruling against the book. (*Times*)

JORDAN

Laith Shubeilat, head of the Engineers' Union and outspoken critic of the government, was released by special amnesty on 8 November. He had been arrested in December 1995 and sentenced to three years' imprisonment the following March on charges of slandering the king and queen (*Index* 3/1996). King Hussein personally informed Shubeilat of his release from Swaqa Prison, south of Amman, and drove him home to his mother's house. The king also promised amnesties to 200 other prisoners arrested during riots in August. (AI)

KAZAKHSTAN

On 5 November President Nursultan Nazarbayev accused trade unions' leaders of 'making trouble during this difficult stage of Kazakhstan's economic transformation'. He was referring to the 'Day of Poverty' demonstrations held in mid-October to protest against the non-payment of wages and pensions totalling US$8.5 million. Nazarbayev also criticised the media for joining the protests and thereby 'violating the constitution and all laws of the state'. (OMRI)

The State Property Committee has notified the country's independent television and radio stations in

Kazakhstan that their contracts with the transmission centre are not valid and will have to be replaced, it was reported on 10 November. Earlier in the month, several independent broadcasters, including **Radio M**, **Totem**, **RIK**, and **KTK TV**, were forced off the air for several days. Officials claim that the stations are broadcasting on frequencies that interfere with air traffic control, but many of the stations have been using their frequencies for four years without complaint. Independent journalists fear that the government is planning to auction all their frequencies to the highest bidder. (OMRI)

KENYA

On 21 November the High Court in Nairobi ordered *Finance* magazine to stop publishing allegedly libellous articles concerning Kuria Kanyingi, chair of the Kiambu branch of the ruling Kenya African National Union (KANU). The case concerned an article published in the 15 October issue which said 'the self-imposed chairman of the ruling party in Kiambu District is behind and involved in criminal activities in the district.' The allegation was repeated in the following issue. (NDIMA)

The Controller of State Houses, Franklin Bett, is suing the *Daily Nation* over an article in its 13 November edition. The article, by chief parliamentary reporter **Emman Omari**, was entitled 'KANU Faction Demands Poll' and referred to Bett as a

member of the 'KANU A' faction. (NDIMA)

Kenyan television cameraman **Mohamed 'Mo' Amin**, widely acclaimed for bringing Ethiopia's famine to world attention in 1984, died aboard the hijacked Ethiopian Airlines Boeing 767 which crashed into the sea just off the Comoro Islands on 23 Noember. Amin, who worked for Reuters Television, was regarded as one of Africa's top photo-journalists. (Reuters)

Koigi wa Wamwere (*Index* 2/1995, 6/1995, 2/1996, 5/1996, 6/1996) was released on bail on 13 December and permitted to travel to London for treatment for a serious heart condition. (Reuters)

Recent publication: *Shadow Justice* (African Rights, December 1996, 267pp)

KYRGYZSTAN

The state publishing house Uchkun refused to print the 9 October issue of the independent newspaper *Res Publica*. Uchkun claimed *Res Publica* owes it 10,000 som (US$800). The paper, however, claims that the government daily *Slovo Kyrgyzstana* owes Uchkun 370,000 som (US$30,000) but continues to be printed nonetheless. *Res Publica*'s editor-in-chief Zamira Sydykova says his paper frequently has problems with Uchkun. (OMRI)

LEBANON

A one-day general strike was called and hundreds of people

demonstrated in Beirut on 28 November against prime minister Rafiq Hariri's government's policies, including the new media law which was due to close over 200 private broadcasting stations by 30 November (*Index* 6/1996). Seventy people were arrested. The protest, called by unions, students, journalists and opposition parties, also demanded the lifting of the three-year ban on demonstrations. The shutdown of the broadcasters was postponed indefinitely until a new licensing system is in place. (Reuters)

An English-language newspaper, the *Beirut Daily Star* which closed 10 years ago, resumed publication in November. Editor-in-chief and publisher is Jamil Mroue, son of Kamel Mroue who founded the paper in 1952 and ran it until he was assassinated in his office in 1966. The paper was forced to close during the civil war. (*Middle East Times*)

MALAWI

In his opening address to the Media Institute of Southern Africa's annual conference, Presdent Bakili Muluzi said that he was 'saddened and concerned' by some of the stories that appear in the Malawian press. 'Their reckless disregard of truth and professional ethics...puts me and others under terrific pressure in our defence of the press,' he said. (MISA)

MALAYSIA

In late October the prime

minister announced his intention to introduce marriage identity cards to married Muslims after several embarrassing cases of mistaken identity. In recent months a number of Muslim couples have been wrongfully detained by the religious police under the Islamic law governing *khalwat*, or close proximity. At the same time film producer Julie Dahlan was accused of committing *khalwat* with her production manager, Rudy Rasiman (a non-Muslim), in a hotel in Tanjung Tokong on 6 October, whilst another member of her crew, Rashidah Dawood, was also accused of committing the same crime with Wirman Buyongsidi at the same location. Dahlan, Dawood, and Buyongsidi will all stand trial on 16 December. (*Straits Times*)

In early November pornographic films and publications were destroyed in an open burning session at the Civil Defence Headquarters attended by the deputy home minister and the film censorship chairman. The burning was condemned by the government a week later, on enviromental grounds. (*Malaysia Business Times*)

The Second Asia-Pacific Conference on East Timor ended abruptly on 9 November when a hundred youths, styling themselves the Malaysian People's Action Front, burst into the conference room. The youths forced their way into the room some 20 minutes after proceedings had begun,

jostling and shouting at delegates, overturning chairs and ripping down banners. The police, who arrived an hour later, first dispersed the mob, then detained the conference's 47 foreign participants. Having issued an order for the remaining 59 delegates to leave, the police promptly detained them for illegal assembly and refusal to disperse. Those held, including 10 Malay journalists and foreign correspondents, were released on 12, 13, and 14 November. (AI, CPJ, Reuters)

The recent bans and restrictions on video arcades and karaoke lounges (now confined to private clubs) in Selangor are to be copied in other states. Both Johor and Pahang announced plans in mid-November to impose tough regulations on entertainment outlets. The most stringent proposals come from Pahang, where karaoke clubs, pubs, and nightclubs in 'Malay-dominated areas' are to be closed and legislation banning Muslim women from working as hostesses in bars is being drafted. (*South China Morning Post*)

Under legislation introduced on 26 November thousands of illegal satellite dishes are to be replaced by those approved by the Information Ministry. Dish owners who do not comply face a fine and possible jail sentence. (*Malaysia Business Times*)

MAURITANIA

The weekly *Le Calame* was banned from publishing for

three months by the Interior Ministry on 26 October. The official reason was that the publication had been 'harming state interests'; other sources point to an interview with a German election observer who questioned whether the elections had been fair. (RSF)

The 8 December issue of the French-language weekly *La Tribune* was seized by the Interior Ministry for reprinting an article from a US paper on slavery in Mauritania. (RSF)

MEXICO

On 12 October **Jesus Ramírez Cuevas**, Reuters correspondent in Chiapas, **Martin Reyes Gutiérrez**, an independent videographer, and **Mauricio Laguna Berber**, correspondent for the magazine *La Crisis*, were detained for more than two hours and threatened with death by a group of men in Mexico City. The journalists had just finished covering the First National Indigenous Congress, which took place from 8–12 October in the capital and in which a representative from the Zapatista National Liberation Army (EZLN) had participated. (RSF, OMCT, Reuters)

Juan Salgado, a member of the Human Rights Academy, received an anonymous death threat on 24 October. Salgado has been active in a campaign to stop the numerous death threats against workers at the **Agustin Pro-Juarez Human Rights Centre** (PRODH). On 9 November Digna Ochoa, a lawyer for

PRODH, was approached by a man who handed her a note containing death threats against her colleagues Pilar Noriega, Enrique Flota, José Lavanderos Yanez and Digna Ochoa and David Fernández Davalos. (AI, OMCT)

On 26 October **Martin Enrique** and **Filiberto Lastra**, reporters for the **Radio XEVA** programme *Telerreportaje*, were beaten with sticks by three armed men in Villahermosa. One of their assailants was Solis Brito, legal adviser for the Tabasco state Department of Public Security. *Telerreportaje* is well known for its critical reporting. (AI)

The Chiapas office of the **Co-ordination of NGOs for Peace** (CONPAZ) was ransacked and burned on 4 November, the fourth such attack in two months. The same night the organisation's chair, Geraldo Gonzales Figueroa, received several death threats and another CONPAZ employee, Javier López Montoya, was abducted with his wife and children by several unidentified men. They were held for 48 hours, during which time they were beaten and threatened with death if Javier López continued working with the organisation. CONPAZ has been particularly critical of the government's failure to stop human rights violations in Chiapas and has brought cases against the army to the Inter-American Commission on Human Rights. (AI, CONPAZ)

Edgar Mason Villalobos, an

economist and correspondent for the daily *El Financiero* and the radio programme *Usted Que Opina*, was murdered at his home in Cuernavaca on 28 November. He was shot in the head with a .38 calibre pistol. (IAPA)

MOROCCO

Jacques de Barrin, a journalist on French daily *Le Monde*'s foreign desk, was refused permission by the Information Ministry to visit Morocco to cover a referendum in September. (RSF)

The ban on the French weekly *Jeune Afrique*, in force since November 1995, has been lifted. (RSF)

NAMIBIA

The attorney-general, Reinhard Rukoro, has said he plans to appeal against the September 1996 High Court ruling that section 11 of the **Racial Discrimination Prohibition Act** is 'invalid' because it violates the constitutional right to freedom of expression (*Index* 6/1996). (MISA)

NIGERIA

On 13 October the editor of the opposition *National Concord*, **Dele Alake**, escaped unhurt when five men attempted to ambush him as he left the paper's offices in Lagos. On the same evening, **Richard Akinnola**, the *National Concord*'s law correspondent, was arrested by security agents. He is believed to have been taken to the

State Security Service office on Awolowo Road, although his whereabouts have not been officially confirmed. (Independent Journalism Centre)

On 19 November the lawyers **Gani Fawehinmi** and **Femi Falana** were released after being held without charge since January and February 1996 respectively (*Index* 4/1996). Fawehinmi was the main lawyer for Ken Saro-Wiwa during his trial, as well as representing Nosa Igiebor, editor of *Tell* magazine, who was also detained and released earlier in the year (*Index* 2/1996). (CPJ)

Contrary to previous reports, **Okina Deesor**, a producer for Radio Rivers, has not been released by the authorities after broadcasting the Ogoni national anthem on 18 July. Arrested on 31 July, he remains in custody and is reported to be in ill health (*Index* 6/1996). (CCPJ)

Recent publications: *Guerrilla Journalism* by Michèle Maringues (RSF, 1996, 127pp); *Human Rights Defenders Under Attack* (AI, November 1996, 28pp); *Time to End Contempt for Human Rights* (AI, November 1996, 29pp)

PAKISTAN

In October the offices of *Ummat* were raided and copies of the newspaper burned. The raid was carried out by members of Jamiat Ulema Islam (JUI) in retaliation for an article criticising the Taliban movement. The paper has continued to receive threatening phone calls. (Pakistan Press Foundation)

In an article published on 15 November, *Dawn* accused the authorities of censoring and delaying incoming and outgoing e-mail messages passing through Paknet, a subsidiary of the state-owned Pakistan Telecommunication Corporation (PTC). Agents of the Federal Investigation Agency (FIA) and the Intelligence Bureau (IB) have been posted in the PTC offices to censor e-mail messages. (Pakistan Press Foundation, *Dawn*)

The bail application of imprisoned journalist **Farhan Efendi**, Hyderabad correspondent for *Parcham*, was rejected for a second time at the end of November. He was detained by paramilitary forces on 14 September 1995 and charged with involvement in terrorist activities. (Pakistan Press Foundation)

Ten men attacked the offices of the *Muslim* in Peshawar on 3 December, apparently in retaliation for a cartoon depicting the actress Mussarat Shaheen. The men ransacked the office, smashed equipment and beat senior reporter Fakhr Alam with iron bars. (Pakistan Press Foundation)

Recent publication: *The 'Disappearance' of the Ansari Family* (AI, November 1996, 4pp)

PHILIPPINES

In early October human rights activists were barred from entering the country in a security crackdown for the Asia-Pacific Economic Co-operation (APEC) forum in November. More than one hundred East Timorese were turned away at Manila airport on 7 October on suspicion that they planned to disrupt the forum. Later in the month President Ramos confirmed the existence of an immigration blacklist banning the entry of those whose presence might cause 'disharmony' and 'endanger national security'. Those blacklisted included **Marcelo** and **Luisa Perreira**, co-authors of a book on abuses in East Timor, and **José Ramos-Horta**, joint winner of the 1996 Nobel Peace Prize, who had been invited to speak at a human rights conference planned to coincide with the APEC meeting. Those within Manila who did demonstrate against APEC found their march blocked by police. (Reuters, *Melbourne Age, Guardian*)

Recent publication: *Not Forgotten — The Fate of the Disappeared* (AI, November 1996, 29pp)

POLAND

On 16 October the government's socio-economic committee approved a draft language law drawn up by the Culture Ministry, stipulating that labels on commodities and shop signs be in Polish. The draft law, intended to replace a 1945 decree making Polish the state language, must be approved by the legislative committee before it goes to Parliament. English and German influences on the language have been criticised by language experts. (OMRI)

Television show host **Wojciech Cejrowski** is to be investigated for 'publicly defaming' President Aleksander Kwasniewski. At an event organised by the non-parliamentary opposition Movement for Poland's Reconstruction on 5 November, Cejrowski is reported to have said: 'Kwasniewski, who can't always stand straight on his legs, is profaning the presidential office with his fat ass'. If convicted Cejrowski could be imprisoned for between six months and eight years. (OMRI)

ROMANIA

On 24 October two employees from the independent daily paper *Ziua* were found guilty of libel against authority. **Tana Ardeleanu**, an investigative reporter, and **Sorin Rosca-Stanescu**, managing director, were jailed for 14 and 12 months respectively, well above the six-month sentences requested by the prosecution. They were also stripped of their rights to practise journalism while incarcerated. Charges were first brought in summer 1995 (*Index* 4/1995) in connection with articles claiming that President Iliescu had been recruited by the KGB when a student in Moscow, that he had ordered arms and ammunition to be distributed to the population in December 1989, and was thus responsible for the deaths of more that 1,000 people. (CPJ, IFJ, SWB)

Captain Constantin Bucur, a former employee of the Romanian Intelligence Service (SRI), is to be tried for handing over tapes with classified information to the media, it was reported on 26 October. Bucur was dismissed by the SRI earlier in the year, after producing tapes that he claimed were illegal wiretaps. They contained recordings of conversations by prominent politicians and journalists. (Reuters)

The European Institute for the Media (EIM) reported on 4 November that despite the presence of private media, coverage of the election campaign was unbalanced and favoured the PDSR. The OSCE said that the elections themselves had been free and reasonably fair, but with room for improvement. (EIM, Reuters)

Recent publications: *Sudden Rage at Dawn — Violence Against Roma in Romania* (European Roma Rights Center, September 1996, 62pp); *Ill-Treatment of Minors* (AI, October 1996, 7pp); *Open Letter to the President, the Government and Members of Parliament* (AI, November 1996, 8pp)

RUSSIAN FEDERATION

Russia: Customs officers confiscated 1,505 copies of a report by the Norwegian environmental group **Bellona** (*Index* 3/1996) on the threat

of radiation posed by the Russian northern fleet. The report was being sent to the St Petersburg human rights group Civil Control. (SWB)

Former Soviet dissident **Vladimir Bukovsky** (*Index* 1/1972, 2/1974, 2/1977) has reportedly been denied a visa to travel to Russia from Britain. He was scheduled to meet journalists in St Petersburg on 18 November to voice his support for **Aleksandr Nikitin** (*Index* 5/1996), charged with high treason for his part in researching the Bellona report. (SWB)

The television station **Oryolinform** was ordered to cease broadcasting by the governor of Oryol, Yegor Stroyev, at the end of November. The station has been highly critical of Stroyev, who has refused to allow Oryolinform journalists to attend his press briefings. (*Ekspress-Khronika*)

Chechnia: The Russian writer **Nikolay Ivanov**, who was seized and held to ransom by armed rebels, was released on 13 October and allowed to return to Moscow. (SWB)

The separatist station **Presidential TV** returned to the air on 16 October after its director, Salman Betelgireyev, was released by Russian border troops in exchange for a group of captured Russian soldiers. (SWB)

On 4 November 5,000 copies of the book *Chechnia — The Struggle for Freedom* by President Zelimknan

Yandarbiyev were seized at the Ukrainian-Russian border. (SWB)

Recent publication: *Torture and Ill-Treatment* (AI, October 1996, 14pp)

RWANDA

On 11 November around 30 foreign journalists were ordered out of Goma in eastern Zaire by rebel forces. A rebel commander who identified himself as Commandant Joseph cited security concerns as the reason. (Reuters)

Recent publication: *Broadcasting Genocide — Censorship, Propaganda and State-Sponsored Violence in Rwanda 1990-1994* (A19, October 1996, 180pp)

SERBIA-MONTENEGRO

Montenegro: Podgorican authorities are threatening not to extend the broadcasting licence of **Antenna M**, the only independent radio station in Montenegro. The station also carries programming from Serbia's Radio B-92. (Radio B-92)

Serbia: On 18 October **Milovan Brkic**, a Serbian investigative journalist for the monthly *Srpska Rec* and Serbian Renewal Movement candidate for the Belgrade city assembly, was assaulted in his office by state security policemen, apparently in connection with an article examining links between state security and organised crime. (CPJ, SWB, OMRI)

The Belgrade station **Radio**

B-92, the student station **Radio Index** and **Radio Boom 93** all suffered frequent interruptions to their transmissions in the days following 27 November. The three stations were the only broadcast media to report on the street demonstrations in Belgrade and Nis against the government's annulment of the municipal elections. The stations were banned outright on 3 December but, following international protests, B-92 and Index were allowed to resume broadcasting three days later. Boom 93 is still off the air. The government blamed the stations' absence from the airwaves on 'heavy rains' knocking out their transmitter. During the ban, Radio B-92 broadcasts were made available over the Internet. (Reuters, SWB)

The Yugoslav Federal Inspector for Traffic and Communications on 1 December banned five radio stations in Cacak, where the opposition initially won a majority of votes in the municipal elections. The stations are **Radio Ozon**, **Radio Soliter**, **Dzoker Radio**, **Radio 96** and **Star FM**. (Radio B-92)

Blic, a new independent daily which gave front-page coverage to the anti-government protests said the state-run printing works, Borba, had pressed for its print-run to be cut to 70,000 from its usual 230,000. On 27 November 40 reporters walked out in protest over a commentary due to be published on 29 November apologising for the paper's coverage of the

protests. Also on 27 November the deputy editor-in-chief, Cvijetin Milivojevic, resigned following the owner's decision to cut political coverage. (IFJ, Reuters, SWB)

SIERRA LEONE

Charges against **Edison Yongai**, editor of the *Point*, for sedition and libel in a July article entitled 'Corrupt Ministers' were dropped prior to his hearing scheduled for 10 October (*Index* 5/1996, 6/1996). (CPJ)

On the morning of 9 October, five newspaper vendors were detained by police in Freetown. They were released that evening, having been neither interrogated nor given any reasons for their detention. This was repeated the following day at Harbour police station. When questioned, the inspector general of police claimed he knew nothing about the incidents, and ordered the release of the second batch of vendors. (CPJ)

Max Jimmy, a staff writer for *Expo Times*, was beaten by officers from the Special Security Department on 9 October after he attempted to interview vice-president Joe Demby. (CPJ)

Sheka Parawali, the editor of *Torchlight* (*Index* 6/1996), was sentenced to one month's imprisonment for contempt of Parliament on 11 October. The charges arose from a story published on 8 October entitled 'Kabbah Bribes MPs'.

Torchlight's owner, the Rev YM Koroma MP, has withdrawn his financial support from the daily and requested that the information minister withdraw its publishing licence. Parawali plans to continue publishing *Torchlight*, but the paper's printer is refusing to carry on printing it. (CPJ)

On 12 October **Hilton Fyle**, editor of the weekly *1 2 3*, pleaded not guilty to three counts of 'publishing a false report likely to cause alarm' and was released on bail of 10 million leones (US$10,000). The charge arose from a 7 October story alleging that justice officials had accepted bribes to drop a fraud case against a former foreign minister and a businessman. (CPJ)

The editor of *Expo Times*, **Gibril Koroma**, and staff writer **Max Jimmy** appeared before Parliament on 5 November to answer charges of contempt of Parliament. They pleaded not guilty, standing by their article of 29 October alleging government involvement in loans by commercial banks to MPs to buy Mercedes Benz vehicles for personal use. On 15 November the pair appeared before the Privileges Committee of Parliament, where they again pleaded not guilty. (CPJ)

The Sierra Leone Association of Journalists has issued a statement of concern about press restrictions, calling government reactions to journalists' investigations 'disproportionate and inappropriate'. A **Media Practitioners Act** is currently being debated in Parliament and would, if passed, establish a Press Council and introduce a system of self-regulation to replace government licensing. (*West Africa*, Sierra Leone Association of Journalists)

SLOVAKIA

The independent daily paper *Sme* was found guilty on 6 November of slandering the Slovak Cabinet, in connection with its reporting of comments made by journalist **Peter Toth** at the funeral of Robert Remias, a former police officer with intelligence connections who was killed in a car bomb in April last year. While dismissing slander charges against Toth himself, the court ruled that *Sme* had quoted him out of context and thereby implicated the government in Remias' death. The paper's publisher was ordered to pay 7.5 million Slovak crowns (US$ 250,000) to the government, 500,000 crowns to prime minister Vladimir Meciar, 450,000 crowns to each of the three deputy premiers, and 400,000 crowns to each of the remaining 14 government members. *Sme* is appealing the verdict. (CPJ)

SOUTH AFRICA

Several journalists were accused of writing 'inaccuracies and lies' at a press briefing held by the anti-drug vigilante group People Against Gangsterism and Drugs (PAGAD) in Cape Town on 6 November. The journalists were paraded through a hostile crowd by PAGAD activists. PAGAD has since called for a boycott of two of the journalists' newspapers, the *Cape Times* and the *Argus*. (MISA, Freedom of Expression Institute)

SOUTH KOREA

Some 444 students were tried for their part in the Yonsei University protest in trials running throughout November (*Index* 6/1996). A total of 225 were found guilty of illegal protest, violence, and obstructing the police and sentenced to between eight months and two-and-a-half years in prison. Two-year suspended sentences were also handed down. (Reuters)

The main opposition party, the National Congress for New Politics (NCNP), accused the government of censoring an article in the weekly *Sisa Journal* on South Korean aid to North Korea. According to NCNP, the government ordered *Sisa* to suspend all printing of the 28 November issue of the magazine and to remove those already produced from sale. (SWB)

On 4 December the government warned that people who log into a website run by North Korea's government could face jail if they download and distribute the material on it. However, it denied reports that Internet Service Providers had been asked to block access to the site. (Reuters)

Recent publication: *Summary of Concerns on Torture and Ill-Treatment* (AI, October 1996, 14pp); *Mass Ill-Treatment of Students in August 1996* (AI, November 1996, 7pp)

TAIWAN

New York Daily News correspondent **Ying Chan** and Taiwanese investigative reporter **Hsieh Chung-liang** are being sued for criminal libel in connection with an article in the 28 October issue of *Yazhou Zhoukan* (Asia Weekly), alleging that the ruling Kuomintang's business manager, Liu Tai-ying, had offered a donation of US$15 million to President Clinton's re-election campaign. Charges of criminal libel are routinely used in Taiwan as a means of stifling independent journalism. If found guilty Hsieh could face two years in jail and Ying could be jailed if she visits Taiwan. For more information see http://www.yingchan.com/. (RSF)

THAILAND

Seven people died and dozens were injured in violence during the run-up to the 17 November parliamentary elections. The electoral monitoring group, Pollwatch, reported an increase in irregularities, including reports of ballot-stuffing in some rural areas, more than US$1 billion spent in vote-buying, and coercion and intimidation by armed and uniformed men. Election winner Chavalit Yongchaiyudh and his New Aspiration Party won most of their seats in the rural northeast, where Thailand's patron-client political corruption is at its worst. They also draw on support from armed forces. (*Far Eastern Economic Review, Guardian*)

TIBET

On 25 October **Ngawang Tharchin** was sentenced to a three-year term of 're-education through labour'. Ngawang had interrupted a lecture by a well-known Tibetan historian during the re-education campaign at Drepung monastery (*Index* 5/1996). Another Drepung monk, **Gyaltsen Yeshe**, is also believed to be serving a three-year sentence for a similar offence. Three other members of Drepung monastery — **Yeshe Changchub, Ngawang Choegyal,** and **Jampel Wangchug** — are believed to have been in detention since August. And **Ngawang Sangdrol**, a nun being held in Lhasa's Drapchi prison, has had her six-year sentence increased to 15 years for disrupting a prison re-education drive. Ngawang refused to stand in the presence of a prison official and shouted 'Free Tibet' during a punishment session. (Tibet Information Network)

Artist **Yungdrung** was released on 27 October after 58 days in custody in Lhasa. Yungdrung, who was reportedly tortured during detention, is believed to have been detained in connection with his portraits of the Dalai Lama, whose image has been banned in Tibet since 5 April (*Index* 4/1996). Yungdrung's home was also raided and his paintings confiscated. (Tibet Information Network)

Members of the European Parliament visiting Tibet in early November reported that the leading dissident and lama, **Yulo Dawa Tsering**, appears to be under house arrest in Lhasa. The MEPs, who were only permitted to see Yulo for 10 minutes, described how he appeared to be 'under some kind of restraint without freedom to come and go'. The lama, who has spent 27 years in jail, is apparently being punished for speaking to a UN human rights team that visited Tibet two years ago. (Tibet Information Network)

TONGA

On 14 October **Kalafi Moala, Filo 'Akau'ola** and **'Akilisi Pohiva** were released from prison after serving 24 days of their 30-day sentence for contempt of Parliament (*Index* 6/1996). The Chief Justice ruled that the Legislative Assembly had breached several constitutional provisions in convicting the trio, and that they had therefore been detained illegally. On 15 November, however, 'Akau'ola, deputy editor of the *Times of Tonga*, was again questioned by police, and pro-democracy politicians 'Akilisi Pohiva and Teisina Fuko were detained overnight at a police station on sedition charges stemming from newspaper articles calling for greater democracy. (Pacific Islands News Association, AI)

TUNISIA

Human rights lawyer **Najib Hosni**, arrested in June 1994

(*Index* 6/1994), was acquitted of charges of arms possession and terrorism on the grounds of lack of evidence. However, he remains in jail after being found guilty on an earlier charge of 'falsification of a land contract'. He is believed to have been tortured while being held at the Ministry of the Interior. (AI)

TURKEY

On 18 October the trial of 48 police officers accused in the murder of journalist **Metin Göktepe** in Istanbul on 8 January (*Index* 2/1996) began in Aydin. (RSF, Reuters)

On 18 October an appeals court confirmed the 20-month suspended sentence given to the writer **Yasar Kemal** for 'inciting racism' in his articles 'The Dark Cloud Over Turkey' and 'More Oppression' (*Index* 3/1996). (Reuters)

On 6 November **Filiz Kocali**, editor-in-chief of the women's monthly *Pazartesi*, and **Arzu Erkol**, a journalist with the left-wing weekly *Atilim,* were detained by anti-riot police while covering a student demonstration in Istanbul. No official source has confirmed the arrest of Kocali and Erkol, causing concern for their safety. (RSF)

On 15 November journalist **Ahmet Altan** went on trial in Istanbul charged under Article 159 of the penal code with insulting the army. The case arose from two articles by Altan in the mass-circulation *Yeni Yüzel* (New Century) on Turkey's 12-year old conflict with Kurdish guerrillas. Altan is also one of the 98 writers and intellectuals who have signed up and are currently on trial as publishers of the book *Freedom of Thought in Turkey* (*Index* 6/1996). (Reuters, PEN)

On 19 November **Osman Murat Ülke**, head of the now defunct Izmir War Resisters' Association, appeared in court charged under Article 155 of the penal code which bars 'all propaganda aiming to break national strength and alienate the public from the military'. In 1995 Ülke publicly burned his military draft documents. Turkish laws do not allow for conscientious objection to military service, which is compulsory for up to 18 months for every Turkish male from 20 years of age. Several other members of the Association, and members of peaceful religious movements have been jailed in the past for refusing to do national service. (Reuters)

Following a much-publicised car crash at the beginning of November in which a wanted gangster, a top policeman and a former beauty queen died, the government threatened in mid-November to tighten up existing press laws. Media probes into the accident have raised serious questions about connections between the state and organised crime. The justice minister, Sevket Kazan, told Parliament: 'We want to bring the issue of lies in the media under control.' The government subsequently brought in new legislation to

prevent the publication of material that 'undermines the credibility of the state or causes public panic through false or unfounded information'. Almost 1,700 journalists signed a petition on 26 November protesting against the new law. (Reuters)

On 22 November the Justice Ministry stopped a group of Italian lawyers from entering Ankara's Central Prison to present jailed Kurdish MP **Leyla Zana** with honorary citizenship of the city of Rome. She is currently serving a 15-year prison sentence for speaking Kurdish in the Turkish Parliament. (Reuters)

Recent publications: *Children at Risk of Torture, Death in Custody and 'Disappearance'* (AI, November 1996, 31pp)

UGANDA

On 13 November, the High Court rejected an appeal by **Haruna Kanaabi**, editor-in-chief of the Islamic weekly *Shariat*, against his conviction on charges of sedition. Kanaabi is the first journalist to be charged with sedition since Yoweri Museveni came to power in 1986. (CPJ)

On 27 November the senior presidential adviser on the media and public relations, John Nagenda, warned that the government might curtail official advertising and other subsidies to opposition newspapers. Addressing 50 journalists taking part in a course on investigative journalism, Nagenda said that governments all over the world have 'the power to withdraw

favours from papers that undermine them.' (SWB)

Peter Busiku, editor of the weekly *Uganda Express*, was arrested on 4 December and charged with publishing false reports likely to cause fear and alarm to the public. The paper's most recent edition had carried an article alleging Uganda's involvement in the crisis in Zaire. (Uganda Journalists Safety Committee)

UNITED ARAB EMIRATES

In November an Islamic court sentenced a Lebanese Christian, **Elie Dib Ghalib**, to 39 lashes and one year in prison for marrying a Muslim woman who is a UAE national. The court also refused to recognise the validity of their marriage in a Lebanese church. Ghalib was allegedly beaten and flogged many times during his pre-trial detention and interrogation in al-'Ain police station in an attempt to force him to sign a confession. Under Islamic law in the UAE a Muslim woman cannot marry a non-Muslim unless he converts to Islam. Unconfirmed reports suggest the sentence of 39 lashes has not yet been carried out because Ghalib expressed an intention to convert to Islam. (*Times*, Human Rights Actions Network, AI)

UNITED KINGDOM

On 8 November heritage secretary Virginia Bottomley called on local councils to use their powers to prevent the David Cronenberg film *Crash* coming to cinema screens. On 20 November Westminster City councillors responded by banning the film in central London, at least while the British Board of Film Classification decides whether to pass it for viewing. Based on JG Ballard's 1973 novel and dealing with the activities of a group of people who are sexually aroused by car crashes, *Crash* has already drawn large audiences in France and Canada. Bottomley said the film contained 'too much violence and unacceptable behaviour'. (*Guardian, Times, Independent*)

A new satirical television series, *Brass Eye*, fronted by comedian Chris Morris, was pulled by Channel 4, days before its planned screening on 19 November. The channel said that it needed 'more time to revise the series'. The programme-makers had duped several politicians into asking parliamentary questions about a non-existent drug called 'cake', a putative new import from the Czech Republic. Home Office minister Tom Sackville later criticised the 'waste of Home Office time'. (*Guardian, Independent*)

There has been a chorus of calls for tougher restrictions on sex and violence on television and in films in recent weeks. Home secretary Michael Howard has demanded that the British Board of Film Classification submit a report outlining its plans to curb video violence. A call for a national campaign against violence was taken up in most of the popular press, and was followed by a new

set of producer guidelines from the BBC in response to what it called a 'shift in moral values'. In a rebuff to senior BBC correspondent Martin Bell and former World Service chief John Tusa's demands for the full reality of war to be conveyed in news coverage, the guidelines laid down a new tougher line on the depiction of violence both in fiction and factual programming. Sex and profanity were also covered. Meanwhile, heritage secretary Virginia Bottomley met the heads of the BBC, the Independent Television Commission and the Broadcasting Standards Council on 11 December to discuss onscreen violence. (*Times, Guardian, Independent*)

Lord Wakeham, chairman of the Press Complaints Commission, spoke out against press intrusion into the private lives of prominent public figures and announced that the PCC's code of practice in this area would be rewritten. The redrafted code will deal with the use of bugging devices and long-range lenses on private property, subterfuge used in obtaining information, the interviewing or photographing of children, and will tighten the definition of 'public interest'. (*Independent, Guardian, Times*)

A law giving the police new powers to break into homes and offices to install bugging devices and conduct covert searches completed its committee stage in the House of Lords on 2 December. The law can be used in the investigation of 'conduct by a large

number of persons in pursuit of a common purpose', giving rise to fears that it could be used against, for example, political or environmental activists. Authority for the use of bugs may be granted by a chief constable, without applying for a warrant from a judge, and it is not necessary that the subjects of surveillance be under suspicion themselves of being disposed to commit serious crime. This legislation followed a ruling in July, confirming the admissibility of evidence obtained through trespass and bugging. (*Independent, Times*)

A radio advertisement for the Ford Courier van was withdrawn following complaints from mental health charities about its references to schizophrenia. The advertisement featured comedian Alexei Sayle explaining that he was 'in two minds' about whether he wanted a big van or a small van. (*Times*)

Recent publication: *Detention and Imprisonment of Asylum Seekers* (AI, December 1996, 65pp)

USA

Amnesty International, calling for further investigation into training manuals used at the **Army School of the Americas** (*Index 6/1996*), has urged the government to provide the public with actual materials and all relevant information, to assume responsibility for the human rights violations that they say occurred as the result of instruction from the manuals, and to ensure the discontinuation of their use. (AI)

On 10 October the Court of Appeals awarded full First Amendment protection to street artists, who are now free to display and sell their work in public places without a licence. The ruling acknowledges the right to view and buy art on the street as an alternative to galleries and museums, and recognises visual art as a protected form of 'speech' equal to written expression (*Index* 3/1996). (Artists' Response to Illegal State Tactics)

Two more defendants in the case of murdered journalist **Manuel de Dios Unanue** pleaded guilty on 30 October, and were sentenced by a Brooklyn federal court judge. (CPJ)

On 31 October the American Civil Liberties Union (ACLU) filed a motion to the Supreme Court, requesting affirmation of a lower court's ruling which found the **Communications De-cency Act** unconstitutional. The brief was filed in response to the government's appeal of the district court ruling, made in June 1996 (*Index* 2/1996, 3/1996, 5/1996). However in early December the Supreme Court announced that it would hear the government's appeal, which means that it will have to consider the merits of the CDA. Hearings are expected to begin in March or April. (Newsbytes News Network, *Computing*)

On 1 November Philadelphia Common Pleas Court Judge

Albert Sabo ruled Veronica Jones' latest testimony in the case of **Mumia Abu-Jamal** (see page 128) as 'incredible and worthy of little belief'. Jones stated that police had coerced her into falsely testifying against Abu-Jamal in his original trial. Abu-Jamal's defence has appealed Sabo's decision (*Index* 2/1996, 5/1996, 6/1996). (Equal Justice)

On 4 November a US District Court judge granted **America Online** the right to block e-mail from the Philadelphia-based company Cyber Promotions Inc, on the grounds that promotional companies have no First Amendment right to flood the Internet with their material. 'That is not free speech on the Internet', said the president of Cyber, who considers AOL a competitor for advertising. 'It's a very sad day when a few very powerful media companies like AOL can censor free speech for the benefit of their own financial interests.' (Interactive Daily)

The Supreme Court rejected an appeal by Mississippi to reinstate a state law allowing student-led prayer in public schools on 4 November. The law was struck down in 1994 for violating constitutional requirements on the separation between church and state. (Reuters)

Proposition 209, which bans state affirmative action programmes for minority groups in California, was blocked on 27 November by a federal judge. The proposition was

passed in the election on 5 November and the American Civil Liberties Union and other civil rights, business and education groups promptly sued to block its implementation. They claimed it violates the equal protection and supremacy clauses of the US Constitution. (Reuters, *Los Angeles Times*)

Television and film industry chiefs announced a new system of ratings for programmes in mid-December, based on the system already in use for films, which will be used in conjunction with the **v-chip**. The ratings will not apply to news, current affairs or sport programmes. (Reuters)

Recent publication: *All Too Familiar — Sexual Abuse of Women in US State Prisons* (HRW, December 1996, 347pp)

VATICAN CITY

On 24 November Cardinal Joseph Ratzinger, the Catholic Church's prefect of the congregation for the propagation of the faith, urged young people not to listen to rock music, which he termed an 'instrument of the devil', for fear of endangering their souls. Warning against the 'diabolical and satanic messages' contained in some modern heavy metal music, he also mentioned the 'subliminal' satanic influence exercised by more traditional groups such the Beatles, the Rolling Stones, Pink Floyd, Queen and the Eagles. As the highest moral authority in the Church after the Pope,

NOELLE HANRAHAN

Inside death row

THE promise of death is not enough. The state of Pennsylvania wants to still Mumia Abu-Jamal's voice and enforce his silence. On 11 November, the Pennsylvania Department of Corrections banned journalists from having access to the entire prison population, in what inmates have labelled the 'Mumia rule'.

The stark reality of a place where men and women wait for death is a secluded and secretive world. As America gears up for assembly line executions, it must dehumanise its victims. A key component of this strategy is to make these men and women invisible. In an ominous trend, the California Department of Corrections — the largest prison system in the USA — in December 1995 eliminated all media access to prisoners.

Prisoners on death row are allowed just one, two-hour non-contact visit per week and two 10-minute phone calls a month. If prisoners are under investigation for a disciplinary infraction — such as 'engaging in the profession of journalism' — all visits and calls are denied. Intimidation and humiliation are used to discourage visits. Mumia is forced to submit to a full cavity search before and after each, completely non-contact visit. There is a price exacted to see and talk with another human being.

On 31 October, in his last interview before the press ban, Mumia said: 'The guiding theme of this jail is an attack on the life of the mind. To isolate people. To make it easier to kill people. And for some this place creates a desire to leave this life.'

In May 1994 Mumia's battle to be heard intensified when Robert Dole and the National Fraternal Order of Police forced National Public Radio to censor Mumia's regular radio commentaries on *All Things Considered*. The state has eliminated new prison recordings. Ten of his radio essays, some of Mumia's last recordings, remain under lock and key. Although under great pressure to do so, NPR has refused either to air or release them.

'The state would rather give me an Uzi than a microphone,' comments Mumia. And the major networks are complicit in the censorship. No recordings of Mumia's voice have ever been aired on a national network news broadcast.

For more information on Mumia Abu-Jamal's case contact Equal Justice USA/West, 558 Capp St, San Francisco, CA 94110. Tel (415) 648-4505; fax (415) 285-5066; e-mail ejuswest@sirius.com

MUMIA ABU-JAMAL

Capitol punishment

THE death penalty is a creation of the state, and politicians justify it by using it as a stepping stone to higher political office. It's very popular to use isolated cases — always the most gruesome ones — to make generalisations about inmates on death row and justify their sentences. Yet it is deceitful; it is untrue, unreal. Politicians talk about people on death row as if they are the worst of the worst, monsters and so forth. But they will not talk about the thousands of men and women in our country serving lesser sentences for similar and even identical crimes. Or others who, by virtue of their wealth and their ability to retain a good private lawyer, are not convicted at all. The criminal court system calls itself a justice system, but it measures privilege, wealth, power, social status and — last but not least — race, to determine who goes to death row.

Why is it that Pennsylvania's African-Americans, who make up only nine per cent of its population, comprise close to two thirds of its death row population? It is because its largest city, Philadelphia, like Houston and Miami and other cities, is a place where politicians have built their careers on sending people to death row. They are not making their constituents any safer. They are not administering justice by their example. They are simply revealing the partiality of justice.

Let us never forget that the overwhelming majority of people on death row are poor. Most of them cannot afford the resources to develop an adequate defence to compete with the forces of the state, let along money to buy a decent suit to wear in court. As the OJ Simpson case illustrated once again: the kind of defence you get is the kind of defence you can afford. In Pennsylvania, New Jersey and New York, in Florida, in Texas, in Illinois, in California — most of the people on death row are there because they could not afford what OJ could afford, which is the best defence.

One of the most widespread arguments in favour of the death penalty is that it deters crime. Study after study has shown that it does not. If capital punishment deters anything at all, it is rational thinking. How else would it be conceivable in a supposedly enlightened, democratic society? Until we recognise the evil irrationality of capital punishment, we will only add, brick by brick, execution by execution, to the dark temple of Fear. How many more lives will be sacrificed on its altar?

© *Mumia Abu-Jamal Extracted from* Death Blossoms — Reflections from a Prisoner of Conscience *preface by Cornel West, published January 1997 by Plough Publishing House, tel: +1 800 521 8011 (USA) or +44 800 269048 (UK); e-mail: cstober@bruderhof.com*

Ratzinger has a reputation as an arch-conservative. (*Telegraph*)

VIETNAM

The *Far Eastern Economic Review*'s correspondent in Vietnam, **Adam Schwarz**, was refused a new visa and forced to leave Hanoi on 11 November. No reason has been given for the refusal but the Foreign Ministry is believed to be 'generally unhappy' with Schwarz's work. He is the first accredited correspondent to be forced out of the country since the start of licensing in 1990. (*South China Morning Post*)

Ownership of **satellite dishes** is to be restricted to senior government and Communist Party officials, it was reported in late November. The restriction is seen as an effort to prevent 'foreign influence' from seeping through open information channels. (*Bangkok Post*)

ZAMBIA

On 19 November about 10 members of the opposition Zambia Democratic Congress (ZADECO) forced their way into the studios of the state-owned **Zambia National Broadcasting Corporation** (ZNBC) in Kitwe. The ZADECO members were demanding a live appearance to protest the alleged rigging of the 18 November election result. (Zambia Independent Media Association, MISA)

Jowey Mwinga, editor of the *Monitor* newspaper, was interrogated at Lusaka police headquarters on 20 November, following publication of a story quoting opposition politician Dean Mung'omba's demands that the government nullify the 18 November election results 'or face the consequence of their actions'. (Zambia Independent Media Association, MISA)

On 26 November **Kunda Mwila** of the *Post* was threatened with arrest by the chairman of the Electoral Commission, Bobby Bwalya. The threat followed inquiries made by Mwila as to why election results from some polling stations had apparently gone missing for up to one week. (MISA)

Police searched the offices of the *Monitor* at the end of November, and seized computer disks, press releases and documents. The raid coincided with similar searches at the offices of the **Committee for a Clean Campaign** (CCC), the **Inter-African Network for Human Rights and Development** (AFRONET) and the **Zambian Independent Monitoring Team** (ZIMT). Both CCC and ZIMT had declared publicly that the 18 November elections were not free and fair. (ZIMA, MISA, *Times*)

Supporters of the opposition Liberal Progressive Front (LPF) beat and stoned a **ZNBC** crew on 5 December. The crew were covering a police raid on the home of LPF leader Rodger Chongwe. The police were searching for a letter written by Chongwe to President Mandela of South Africa in which he warned of a possible military takeover in Zambia. (MISA)

ZIMBABWE

On 7 November the High Court upheld the conviction of **Trevor Ncube**, the former editor of the *Financial Gazette*, for criminal defamation (*Index* 3/1996). The *Gazette* had appealed against the ruling on the grounds that the fine imposed was too excessive, that the allegations did not amount to criminal defamation and that there was no intent to defame. (MISA)

★★★

General publications: *Human Rights Watch World Report 1997 — Events of 1996* (HRW, December 1996, 383pp)

★★★

Compiled by: Paul Currion, Anna Feldman, Kate Thal (Africa); Kate Cooper, Catriona Mitchell, Dagmar Schlüter (Americas); Nicholas McAulay, Mansoor Mirza, Sarah Smith (Asia); Ann Chambers, Robin Jones, Vera Rich (eastern Europe and CIS); Michaela Becker, Philippa Nugent (Middle East); Charles Peyton (western Europe)

ANNOUNCING THE GALA CHARITY PREMIERE OF

ARTHUR
MILLER'S
TIMELESS
TALE OF
TRUTH ON
TRIAL.

THE
CRUCIBLE

directed by NICHOLAS HYTNER

with DANIEL DAY-LEWIS
WINONA RYDER
PAUL SCOFIELD

To be held in London in mid-February
Date and ticket details to be announced

In aid of Writers and Scholars Educational Trust,
the charity associated with Index on Censorship

Further details from Joe Hipgrave at Index
33 Islington High Street
London N1 9LH
Tel 0171 278 2313
Fax 0171 278 1878

INDEX
ON CENSORSHIP

ARTICLE 19 & HKJA

Hostages to fortune

For the last four years, Article 19, together with the Hong Kong Journalists Association (HKJA), has campaigned for the review and/or removal of certain laws from Hong Kong's statute books before the handover to China. Their aim has been and continues to be an insistence that China preserve Hong Kong's legal commitment to recognise and uphold the fundamental rights set out in the International Covenant on Civil and Political Rights (ICCPR). Their latest joint annual report, China's Challenge, *covers the period 1 July 1995 – 30 June 1996 and refocuses attention on the Chinese government in the hope of establishing a dialogue. It also warns the UK government of the dangers of leaving its present security laws a hostage to fortune in Beijing's hands. The following excerpts pinpoint continuing concerns about freedom of expression*

CHINA DICTATES THE TERMS

THE past year has seen China move into a higher gear to implement its policies on Hong Kong and play out its preparatory tactics for the resumption of sovereignty. Since the electoral reforms proposed by the Governor, Chris Patten, moved ahead, without China's approval, Beijing's policy on Hong Kong has been to 'direct business mainly on our own' (*yi wo wei zhu* literally, making myself the master). China no longer has the political will to work with the British on key transitional issues and is setting the agenda for assuming sovereignty.

Beijing's strident policies on Hong Kong seems to be confirming some darker fears about the continued protection of freedom of expression after 1997. Over the past year the Chinese authorities have shown themselves to be concerned not with protecting the right to freedom of expression, about which they have grave misgivings, but with eroding it.

Several concerns stand out. The first has been moves by the Chinese authorities to weaken legal protections for freedom of expression. In October 1995, the legal sub-group of the China-appointed Preliminary Working Committee (PWC) recommended that sections of the Hong Kong Bill of Rights Ordinance, enacted in the wake of the crackdown in Beijing in 1989, be repealed, and that amendments to six security-related and broadcasting laws be reversed. The reforms to these colonial laws had been made with the intention of bringing them into line with the Bill of Rights.

These recommendations were quickly thrown into sharper relief when China announced its decision to establish a provisional legislature to replace, on 1 July 1997, the existing Legislative Council elected in 1995 under British electoral reforms. Beijing took this decision in the wake of the breakdown of talks with Britain on the composition of the 1995 legislature. China argued that the electoral reforms were contrary to the Sino-British Joint Declaration, the Basic Law, and to past Sino-British understandings on the development of democracy in Hong Kong. The Provisional Legislature is to be elected by the same 400-member Selection Committee that will elect the first chief executive of the Hong Kong Special Administration Region (SAR). However, while the Selection Committee is mandated in the Basic Law to elect the chief executive, there is of course no mention of a provisional legislature, nor any such similar mandate.

With its own, hand-picked legislature in place, even if temporarily, Beijing will be able to ensure that legal effect can be given to its plans to emasculate the Hong Kong Bill of Rights Ordinance and to roll back reforms to restrictive laws which were inconsistent with the Bill of Rights.

Moreover, there are fears that the Provisional Legislature will permit China to set the ground rules under which Article 23 of the Basic Law is brought into force. Under this article, which must be regarded as posing perhaps the greatest constitutional threat to freedom of expression after 1997, the SAR shall enact laws to prohibit, *inter alia,* 'any acts of treason, secession, sedition, subversion against the Central People's Government, or theft of state secrets'.

Parallel to these political developments, the past year has seen mounting pressure on the media from China. Through the local branch of the New China News Agency (Xinhua), China's de facto embassy in Hong Kong, Beijing continues to bring to bear on the local media well-established strategies to persuade organisations and individuals to accept the basic tenets of its policies. Despite Beijing's public reassurances that it will not interfere in the operation of the media after 1997, it is clear from its actions that China is determined to undermine freedom of expression, and that it is already doing so.

LEGISLATIVE REFORMS

THE Preliminary Working Committee's proposed amendments to six security-related and broadcasting laws reverse earlier reforms bringing them into line with the Bill of Rights. The revised laws, as they would be applied after 1 July 1997, are:

• The **Television Ordinance** would allow the authorities, *inter alia,* to pre-censor and prohibit programmes, revoke television licenses for security reasons and stipulate approved sources for news programmes.
• The **Telecommunications Ordinance** would allow the authorities to prohibit radio programmes.
• The **Broadcasting Authority Ordinance** would grant powers to the Broadcasting Authority to vet and prohibit programmes.
• The **Emergency Regulations Ordinance**, notably the **Emergency (Principal) Regulations,** would include subsidiary legislation allowing the executive authorities, *inter alia,* to censor and suppress publications.
• The **Public Order Ordinance** allows the authorities to license public rallies and marches.
• The **Societies Ordinance** would allow the authorities to prohibit links between organisations in Hong Kong and others overseas.

When the PWC concluded its work in December 1995, it had proposed changes to a total of 26 laws, including those above.

THE BILL OF RIGHTS

AS FAR as the Hong Kong Bill of Rights Ordinance is concerned, the past year has been clouded by the recommendations of the PWC to water down the legislation. This proposal was made in a year when fewer cases bringing challenges under the Hong Kong Bill of Rights were taken to the courts, and when judges appeared to be taking a more conservative approach towards such cases.

Since the Hong Kong Bill of Rights came into force in 1991 there have been two principals cases which have centred on the right to freedom of expression under Article 16. The first concerned *Ming Pao* newspaper; the second, concluded in November 1995, ruled that prison authorities were not permitted to remove racing supplements from prisoners' newspapers. Though adjudicating on an unexpected subject, the ruling was to some degree a useful affirmation of the right to freedom of information and one of the few exceptions to the rule in an otherwise less than happy year for the Bill of Rights.

The Hong Kong government's programme to bring laws which are inconsistent with the right to freedom of expression under Article 16 of the Hong Kong Bill of Rights Ordinance (and thereby Article 19 of the ICCPR), or which are otherwise threatening to freedom of expression, remains in an unsatisfactory and unhealthy state. While the government has, over the past year, brought forward some reforms to the powers of the executive authorities to infringe freedom of expression, in many cases these do not go far enough in protecting this fundamental right.

More important, there has been no progress on the reform of contentious security-related legislation since the government, in July 1995, submitted proposals to China for changing them.

Among the security-related laws the HKJA and Article 19 believe should be brought into line with the ICCPR are:

• The **Official Secrets Act,** which prohibits the unauthorised disclosure of information in six broad categories;
• The **Crimes Ordinance,** which defines as seditious the 'intention' of bringing the government into hatred or contempt though any act, publication or speech. This law also contains a broadly-defined crime of treasonable intention. Similarly, the **Post Office Ordinance** prohibits the mailing of seditious publications;
• The **Emergency Regulations Ordinance,** which allows the Governor in Council to declare an emergency in ill-defined circumstances and grants the Governor in Council (and thereby the chief executive of the future SAR) broad powers of censorship.
• Police powers of search and seizure, as set out in the **Interpretation and General Clauses Ordinance,** which, under certain circumstances, permits the authorities to search for and seize journalistic materials gathered in confidence.

Conclusions and recommendations

CONSTITUTIONAL CONCERNS

DISREGARDING the merits of the dispute between China and Britain over electoral reforms, the HKJA and Article 19 are firmly of the view that the proposed Provisional Legislature has no legal basis in the Sino-British Joint Declaration or the Basic Law.

The decision to set up a provisional legislature has important implications for the protection of freedom of expression after 1997. We therefore urge the Chinese authorities to reconsider the establishment of a provisional legislature.

Before the handover, the Provisional Legislature is expected to consider how to give legal effect to recommendations endorsed by the Preliminary Working Committee (PWC) in December 1995 to emasculate the Hong Kong Bill of Rights Ordinance and to reverse amendments made to six security-related and broadcasting laws.

We believe both the PWC recommendation, and the likely follow-up moves to reverse the legal reforms made over the past three years, to be inconsistent with the minimum protections set down in the ICCPR, and with China's obligations under the Sino-British Joint Declaration. As such, any move to introduce these measures would constitute a serious attack on the fundamental right to freedom of expression. We therefore call on the Preparatory Committee to refrain from adopting these or any similar recommendations that breach the protections of freedom of expression guaranteed under international law.

Equally, as the other signatory to the Sino-British Joint Declaration, the British government has a duty to ensure that future constitutional and legal arrangements are consistent with provisions of the bilateral treaty. Although Britain has initiated discussions with the Chinese side on the question of the Provisional Legislature and on the PWC recommendations, there has been little or no progress to date. We believe it is imperative, therefore, that Britain pushes these concerns to the very top of the bilateral transitional agenda, and ensures with China that there are no inconsistencies in the latter's plans for the resumption of sovereignty with the right to freedom of expression as set down in the Sino-British Joint Declaration and the ICCPR.

In both the Sino-British Joint Declaration and the Basic Law, the

Chinese government agreed that the International Covenant on Civil and Political Rights will continue to apply to Hong Kong after 1997. In practice, China remains intransigent on the issue, and has yet to be persuaded by Britain either to accede to the ICCPR in its own right (and, by extension, include Hong Kong) or to agree to allow another mechanism whereby Hong Kong can submit reports directly to the UN Human Rights Committee, as Britain is presently obliged to do under Article 40 of the ICCPR. In order to ensure Hong Kong's human rights record can continue to be monitored after 1997, the HKJA and Article 19 call on China to find an acceptable mechanism by which future periodic reports can be made to the Human Rights Committee.

THE MEDIA

IT IS generally accepted that the right to freedom of expression under the ICCPR does not limit the freedom of a person or organisation to advocate independence or self-determination, so long as this is done peacefully and does not constitute a real and immediate threat to public order or safety. It is incumbent on China, therefore, to further clarify that it is wholly within the rights of the people of Hong Kong to advocate such aspirations if they so wish. The protection of this basic right China has agreed to under both the Sino-British Joint Declaration and the Basic Law.

In April 1996, the China-appointed Preparatory Committee demanded that the government-funded public service broadcast Radio Television Hong Kong (RTHK) give it airtime to publicise its activities. RTHK, which currently enjoys editorial independence, replied in a statement that provision of airtime can only be guaranteed if the station's editorial independence is not compromised. This prompted China to respond that, as it is a government body, RTHK should be disciplined and brought into line. Though the issue remains to be resolved, it has understandably raised considerable fears about the continued autonomy of RTHK after 1997.

A fair part of the blame must lie with the Hong Kong government, which has failed to provide cast-iron guarantees for the future editorial independence of RTHK. Public service broadcasting, if is to serve its twin functions of informing the public and acting as a watchdog of government, must have full guarantees of editorial independence. The Hong Kong government must therefore move urgently to guarantee the independence of RTHK, as recommended in the 1985 review of broadcasting.

At the same time it is also incumbent on China to respect the existing and future editorial independence of this public service broadcaster. We therefore urge China to commit itself to the protection of the independence of the RTHK. In a similar vein, we also urge China to encourage consideration in the Hong Kong SAR to reversing the present Hong Kong government's decision not to allow public access television broadcasting.

The access of the Hong Kong media to China continues to be stringently regulated by the Chinese authorities. Incidents in which Hong Kong journalists working in China have been detained or harassed by mainland officials have increased over the past year. This is a very regrettable development. In a similar vein, we continue to be deeply concerned at the fate of Xi Yang, a Hong Kong-based journalist who is presently in jail in China serving a 12-year sentence for the alleged theft of state secrets. According to accounts from his relatives, Xi Yang's health is deteriorating. The HKJA and Article 19, while continuing to believe that his prosecution was wrong in principle, urge that the Chinese government, in view of his failing health, release him from prison on humanitarian grounds.

ACCESS TO INFORMATION

FINALLY, the HKJA and Article 19 are of the view that the government's present administrative code on access to information, which may be open to differential application by administrators, does not adequately give effect to, and protect, the right to freedom of information. Under Article 16 of the Hong Kong Bill of Rights Ordinance, the Hong Kong government has a duty to enact freedom of information legislation in order to give effect to the public's right of access to official information. We call upon the government urgently to address this issue, either through the introduction of its own bill or by allowing a private member's bill to be introduced into the Legislative Council. ❏

China's Challenge: Freedom of Expression in Hong Kong *(A19 & HKJA, 1996) is available from Article 19, 33 Islington High Street London N1 9LH price £3.99/US$6)*

Hong Kong's challenge 1996: pro-democracy activists in Hong Kong commemorate the Tiananmen Massacre; Credit: Chris Stowers/Panos Pictures

JONATHAN MIRSKY

The way we live now

There's still six months to go, but Beijing's calling the shots already and the territory's busy collaborating

HONG KONG'S political atmosphere is now as poisonous as the city's polluted harbour and about as infectious — not with hepatitis A and B, but with malice. This is not surprising. Something peculiar, maybe unique, is about to happen. One of the most successful colonies ever, which if made independent would eclipse Singapore, will soon be handed over to China, from which most of the colony's population are refugees or the children of refugees.

This is the China which the Berlin-based Transparency International, a non-government institute funded by the UN and the US Agency for International Development, recently pronounced the fifth most corrupt country in the world, just ahead of Nigeria, Pakistan, Kenya, and Bangladesh; Control Risks in London puts China in the top four most dangerous Asian countries for businessmen fearing kidnap, robbery, or murder, just behind Cambodia, Pakistan, and Burma. Amnesty ranks it first in extra-legal executions.

It is another world across the border. Its rulers, in the words of Sir Percy Cradock, Margaret Thatcher's and John Major's ex-China expert, who ceaselessly blames Governor Patten for daring to confront China, 'have always been thugs, are thugs, and always will be thugs'. We are supposed to be getting used to being ruled by these people, whose supporters or sycophants say nothing important is going to change. And yet at 12 midnight on 30 June 1997 the 'future sovereign' will abolish the elected legislature and appoint another, choose its own Chief Executive, water down the Bill of Rights, bring in a garrison which will not be subject to local laws, and decide the most important legal cases, 'matters of state,' in Beijing.

If this were traditional China, in such a crisis we would expect to hear of new-born deformed animals, blighted crops, strangely coloured rain, eclipses, earthquakes and tidal waves — all auguries of social and political evil just around the corner.

But two-headed babies and five-legged goats are no longer available. Instead, when General Liu Zhenwu, who will command Hong Kong's new garrison in 1997, arrived here recently for nine days of consultations about the future, his second visit in five weeks, he met British and Chinese officials and spoke to the press. But he cancelled his appointment with Anson Chan, the Chief Secretary and Acting Governor while Chris Patten was on holiday.

Nor, when he was here in July, did General Liu meet Chris Patten whose spokesman said the prospect of such a meeting had not even been discussed... Five years ago, in the same situation, the general would have posed for photographers in the portico of Government House with the governor of the day.

This is the way we live now in Hong Kong. Sometimes Beijing barks angrily or just murmurs. More often its likes and hatreds are so well understood that, like the colonial cringe of yesteryear, local collaboration with the 'future sovereign' is automatic and pre-emptive. Some taxi drivers now fly little red flags in their front windows. The Dalai Lama arrives in some capital and the presenter of a TV news bulletin abjectly follows Beijing's line, referring to his 'provocative visit'. Not long ago when I asked a friend who presents the news here why items relating to China are either vapid or grovelling she said 'Chinese officials posted here always watch the evening news. If they see something they don't like they call us up immediately. It's incredibly stressful. So we try to prevent the phone calls by doing what they want first.'

Fear of what happens after 1997 lies heavily over the colony. Not long ago seven members of the 60-seat Legislative Council carrying a petition opposing China's plan to abolish the present wholly elected body next year, and to hand-pick 60 new members, were turned away in Beijing. Thirty Hong Kong reporters on the plane, accused of being in league with the councillors, were forced to sign 'self-criticisms'. Within a few days a Legislative Council committee on the media invited each of the 30 to testify on what happened to them; none dared appear. They or their editors feared this would attract Beijing's further anger. Even the pro-Beijing members of the committee were shocked.

Legislator Elizabeth Wong, an outspoken democrat, who was denied a visa in July to address an academic conference in Beijing, says that in the Legislative Council 'some of my colleagues are afraid to look me in the eye. They're afraid of being associated with me.' Ms Wong told me that Hong Kong University, a co-sponsor of the event, was too timid to tell its Beijing counterparts that their behaviour was outrageous.

The higher ranks of the civil service and the police are leaking pre-1997 resignations of experienced men and women not eager to serve the future sovereign. Official spokesmen struggle to explain that the figures are little different from normal 'wastage' and that the departures make room for young, equally able officers. I have never met anyone who believes this.

The Royal Jockey and Royal Golf Clubs dropped 'Royal' from their names over a year before the take-over, and during the debate at the Royal Yacht Club, where the vote narrowly favoured retaining the traditional name, the Commodore, also a high official here, warned that China, the club's future landlord, might resent such a colonial anachronism and make life hard for the yachties.

With two exceptions, Simon Murray of Deutsche Bank and Sir Joseph Hotung, whose private fortune paid for the new China gallery at the British Museum, none of Hong Kong's richest tycoons or company chairmen, including those in the British Chamber of Commerce, speak up publicly for the embattled Governor who is blamed for loss of contracts although no-one can offer a concrete example; indeed British trade with China has risen by at least 16 per cent during the Patten period. Leading local tycoons, such as James Tien, chairman of the Hong Kong Chamber of Commerce, many of them with British gongs eagerly sought in earlier opportunist times, attack the Governor in large newspaper advertisements whose real audience is across the border.

The New China News Agency, Beijing's de facto embassy here, has sent hundreds of letters to local organisations asking how, not if, they are going to celebrate the handover. There are few refusals. One tiny professional association of writers and artists replied 'there is nothing to celebrate.' This reply undoubtedly will be remembered after the take-over.

Nothing is taken at face value. If a business deal with China fails, perhaps because someone else offered a better one, Chris Patten is blamed. A newspaper leader attacking the Hong Kong government for some legitimate reason is now seen as a sell-out to Beijing; if a foreign journalist writes a favourable story about China he is accused of 'doing anything for access'. Only the BBC World Service, with its reputation for fairness, remains immune to the miasma surrounding the media.

Legislative Council member Christine Loh, who for several years attacked Beijing for threatening Hong Kong, says she intends to go to Beijing to 'hold dialogue' with Chinese officials; she is now suspected by most of her democratic colleagues of selling out simply for wishing to speak to Hong Kong's future rulers. Christine Loh is a woman of integrity who has already said she would not serve in a Chinese-appointed Council unless every single present member were appointed. But character and reputation are no longer enough.

Patriotism, which in Beijing is defined explicitly as loyalty to the Party, is now the watchword for creating a post-1997 government. Even British officials find it hard to put an optimistic gloss on this. China established an apparatus for choosing the members of the Legislature to replace the elected one it will abolish on 1 July. In November 1996 the same apparatus 'elected' a Chief Executive to succeed Governor Patten. Most people here wanted the elected Legco to remain and overwhelmingly preferred Chris Patten's successor to be Anson Chan, the Chief Secretary and his deputy. Beijing, which has regarded Hong Kong as a sinkhole of disloyalty since the marches here in 1989 supporting Tiananmen, ignored these wishes, and arranged the 'election' of a poodle, thereby deepening popular cynicism and resignation. The poodle is shipping tycoon Tung Chee Hwa, whose business was rescued from bankruptcy by Beijing loans in the mid-1980s; he declines to explain these arrangements although they suggest that Tung's obligation to China must be considerable.

Tung Chee Hwa's concept of civil liberties, identical to Beijing's, emerged in early December: 'Although human rights groups concerned with Taiwan and Tibet can set up office in Hong Kong, if their work involves advocacy of Taiwanese and Tibetan independence, as a Chinese man I consider this intolerable.' This is precisely the view of Chinese officials who have declared that 'advocating' certain views, especially in the press and especially on Taiwan and Tibet, will be treated as a crime.

The Hong Kong government itself is now so afraid of China that it is covering up a scandal involving a very high official. Members of the Legislative Council, during a debate, openly speculated, as happened in the Commons during the Kim Philby affair, that before his sudden resignation on full pension he may have filtered secret information to the Chinese. Senior officials both here and in London confirm, off the record, that the man is a scoundrel. The Council is now interrogating senior officials, under oath, about the case. But Government House cannot bear the prospect of a collision with China over possible espionage so near the 1997 takeover, nor the prospect of even more civil servants being demoralised because China now knows something about their dossiers. As a result high officials say nothing except that 'it is a personal matter.' No-one in public life believes this, the government is held up to derision, and many civil servants feel ashamed.

In the absence of natural resources, what made Hong Kong develop differently from China were brains, optimism, and the rule of law. Now the benchmark is attitude towards China. Beijing is largely to blame. Its defining words, 'friend,' 'patriotic,' 'love China' and 'enemy,' together with its concept of the law as an instrument of state power, have paralysed sense and numbed sensibility. ❏

Jonathan Mirsky is East Asia editor of The Times

HELEN SIU

Remade in Hong Kong

When China tells Hong Kong to 'Keep on dancing, keep on horse racing', locals ask to what extent 'the people of Hong Kong' can choose to dance to their own tunes?

VISITORS to Hong Kong are often intrigued by the kaleidoscope of cultural images. One feels a nostalgic colonial elegance when sipping afternoon tea at the Peninsula Hotel. Wandering pass the expensive boutique shops at Ocean Terminal, one reaches a mosque standing alongside the barracks for the Ghurkha regiment. Further north is Temple Street, where Cantonese opera, fortune tellers, street hawkers from Nepal, street stores, food stores serving Thai, Vietnamese food all congregate together. If one ventures further, there is 'Women Street' *'neuih yahn gaai'*, a clothing market providing styles and sizes for cadres now visiting from China in tens of thousands.

These multicultural images of Hong Kong are striking today, but parallel images had probably existed even when 'Hong Kong' began in the mid-nineteenth century. Local fishing and farming villages did not transform themselves overnight into a world metropolis. They joined Hong Kong a century later. From the beginning, 'Hong Kong' was an urban commercial experience.

So, today, a walk from the Admiralty up Garden Road takes one past St Joseph's and St Paul's, missionary schools which have provided elite western education to generations of Hong Kong children. Passing the St John's Cathedral and the Governor's residence, one eventually reaches the Indian trading companies, the Victoria prison and the Man Mo Temple along Hollywood Road. Such a walk allows us to wander into history when a racially mixed expatriate community and an equally complicated world of Chinese merchants and labourers became woven together to initiate a multicultural happening we now call Hong Kong.

These images beg the question: Is there a 'Hong Kong' cultural identity? Until recently, it's been difficult to pinpoint 'a Hong Konger'. In fact, it's a 'life and death' issue: until our generation dies, it may be hard to find a 'true Hong Konger' in the cemeteries in Hong Kong. For the deceased who belonged to an older generation, the cultural reference point was the native place in China, real or imagined, carved in stone. Before 1949, the boundary between Hong Kong and the mainland was not a clear one. Shanghai, Guangzhou and Hong Kong were three nodes in a well-traversed regional network of business, capital, people and consumer culture. Items circulated among these cities included theatre groups and their most prized actresses.

The networks applied to working people as well. Over the last two decades, many men 60 and older in the Pearl River Delta have worked in Guangzhou and/or Hong Kong, are informed about the affairs of the outside world and are also socially well connected to Hong Kong and Macau.

However, the links between Hong Kong and China through Guangdong have historically been treated with some ambivalence. Beijing would like to remind regional populations that they owe allegiance to the political centre, but when resourceful southerners have taken their Chineseness seriously, it has meant trouble. Historically, from the Taiping Rebellion in the mid-nineteenth century to Liang Chi-chao, Sun Yat-sen and the tearful protests in Victoria Park in the wake of 4 June 1989, southerners have occasionally taken it upon themselves to challenge the regimes in Beijing. 'Being Chinese' does not involve a fixed set of cultural rules based on primordial origins. Rather, its social and political meanings are subject to constant negotiation at different times and places. Identities can be claimed by some or imposed by others. It often depends on where you are at the negotiating table.

So is there a China problem for a Hong Kong generation today? Or, if we turn the question around, is there a Hong Kong problem for a generation of leaders in China? Historically, events that made Hong Kong culturally porous have posed problems of identity for its residents; the latest landmark is 1997. Understandably, no Chinese official will bear the responsibility of renewing an unequal treaty with Britain. When confronted, the leadership often insists on the integrity of China's

Credit: *Zunzi*

national boundaries and claims the loyalty of those they consider ethnic Chinese. What language one speaks, what social issues one empathises with and whether one decides to own a foreign passport or not, become problems of patriotism and identity.

While one cannot fit an ideological cap on a complex historical process, the question of identity and its political implications have been extremely difficult for an elite generation in Hong Kong now approaching middle-age. This generation is a source of anxiety for Beijing as well. Baby-boomers of the post-war Hong Kong, the western-educated, jet-setting professional backbone of the territory's financial miracle, find themselves not exactly tuned to receive the signals from

China. Behind their pleas for institutional guarantees is a lack of trust in China's political process. For the proponents not to have raised the issue during British rule and to raise it only in anticipation of the change of sovereignty is irksome for Beijing.

Few Hong Kong residents will choose to deny their 'Chinese' ancestry. But if estimates were right — that one out of every six persons marched in the wake of the 4 June incident — their action sends a troublesome message to the Chinese government: cultural identification does not automatically lead to unquestioned political commitment. The feelings of this generation should be better understood. Although the south China/Hong Kong nexus had been strong, the children of those who crossed the border in and around 1949 knew a much less intimate China and a very different Hong Kong.

In the relatively sleepy colonial environment, those bright and hardworking enough were the two per cent who benefited from an elitist and often western education. By the time they graduated from the universities in the late 1960s and early 1970s, the government, having learned a lesson from the riots in China that spilled over the border and triggered long neglected social problems, had made a crucial political decision to invest heavily in Hong Kong's future. For the baby-boomers, the decision to build new infrastructure in Hong Kong created timely opportunities for careers in government and in business. Over the next 20 years, in the increasingly cosmopolitan environment of Hong Kong, this generation matured into the movers and shakers of the 1990s. In a word, Hong Kong left the China orbit and turned to the world on her own almost by default.

Furthermore, as students, the baby-boomers were most exposed to the social political upheavals of the late 1960s worldwide. Triggered by the various student movements ranging from the French student riots in 1968 to the anti-Vietnam War protests in the USA, these Hong Kong students turned their attention to the particular social problems of Hong Kong. Their restlessness in the early 1970s was also fuelled by renewed curiosity about a 'socialist motherland' they hardly knew: their turn to China was motivated less by primordial concerns than by liberal politics worldwide, combined with an almost religious fervour to believe.

The fourth of June 1989 was a traumatic climax to a decade-long disappointment. From the late 1970s, the flood of new immigrants from rural China and their problems of adjustment made this generation in

Hong Kong aware of just how different they were from their 'compatriots' across the border. The ideological bubble collapsed as the baby-boomers gained increased exposure to the daily workings of the mainland. But by the time they had discovered this, their futures were already tied to the mainland.

Their cultural reference points are as ambiguous as their political orientations. Affiliation with things timelessly Chinese has not come as naturally for them as for their parents. These baby-boomers were as well versed in Shakespeare and TS Eliot as in Tang poetry. From the 1970s on, they put their mark on Canto-pop and set new directions in film-making and so on. Their new art forms signalled a definite departure from the highly moralistic cultural world of the Chinese diaspora, expressing the aspirations of a generation uniquely made in Hong Kong for whom China could no longer provide a reference point.

The careers of these baby-boomers also mirror Hong Kong's projection into the world as the financial metropolis of Asia Pacific. Family businesses have turned global and entered China as well. The post-war generation now occupies key positions in the business world and in government; scholars have defined them as Hong Kong's 'new global middle class'.

> **Whether Hong Kong can maintain its multiple roles as a world metropolis and regional financial centre while becoming an essential part of China, depends a great deal on the mutual accomodations of the local born with these groups who eventually will take root in Hong Kong**

To sum up: they are visible, they are vocal, they are self confident. But life is more than conspicuous consumption. Their intellectual property, their global resources, their financial 'savvy' and, last but not least, their social awareness, make Beijing both envious and uncomfortable. It will not be easy for the Chinese government to claim their cultural identity or tempt them with purely economic gain. Unlike previous generations, this one is most actively involved in the region's future and has the most to lose if the opening of China and the transition in Hong Kong become problematic. At the same time, the baby-boomers are eager to face China on their own terms.

BUT we are increasingly faced with another social group, equally important for China's future. As the 1970s saw the post-war Hong Kong generation consolidating itself as the visible social force, a new wave of immigrants from China began their sojourn. Hong Kong has always been a land of immigrants and emigrants, but the term 'new immigrant' that emerged to describe this particular wave of immigrants in the late 1970s, glosses over a fluid and complex social-political process that has a great deal to do with the interaction between these two groups. The adjustment of these immigrants into a highly volatile Hong Kong has been harsh. They came at a time when the local-born were beginning to be anxious about their future. From the early 1980s on, the terms '*ah chaam*' or '*daaih hyunjái*' became household words for poor, country-bumpkins and underworld crime.

While the intolerance of professional circles towards the so-called new immigrants might have arisen from imagined encroachment from China, those from the working class felt the real threat to their livelihoods. And this came at a time when manufacturing was beginning to move out of Hong Kong across to the Pearl River Delta. These derogatory images of the new immigrants became ways for the local born in Hong Kong to draw boundaries between 'us' the residents of Hong Kong and 'them' the outsiders.

Nevertheless, the step by step economic liberalisation of China from the early 1980s on brought unprecedented opportunities for the various newcomers to Hong Kong. Those with skills and contacts rapidly became the crucial links between businesses in Hong Kong and China. Foreign and joint ventures employ millions in Guangdong and the means for linking up with local power structures remain important for business. In this respect, new immigrants returning from Hong Kong are best placed to be economic and political brokers. They are the regular commuters on the trains and the river boats to Guangzhou and the Delta, a vital part of the process of reintegration.

The return of these new immigrants has also had profound effects in Guangdong. The influx of wealth, consumer goods and exposure to popular Hong Kong TV is moulding a local population that identifies less with the ideological machinery in Beijing and more with soap operas on Hong Kong TV.

'Hong Kong people running Hong Kong' (*Gong yahn jih gong*) is not an empty slogan, but one needs to take a closer look at the range of Hong

Kong residents, from the local born to the various waves of immigrants. Upward mobility for the baby-boomers meant the refinements of a cosmopolitan culture and a professional ethic. It enabled a generation to join an affluent global community. But, in the past decade, the social mobility of the new immigrant in Hong Kong has been intimately tied to the explosion of speculation and the manoeuvres of a relatively deprived population in post-Mao China. Lavish banqueting and fancy karaoke bars are some of the more popular symbols of the good life on the fast track. In the boom towns along the dirt roads in the Delta, one also finds an increasing number of Mercedes with Guangdong/Hong Kong licence plates taking the new breed of political brokers to their factories. On the streets of Hong Kong, one finds smartly dressed cadres loudly in command with their cellular phones.

The rise of the new immigrant entrepreneurs readily tuned to China is coupled with the ever increasing presence of mainland officials in Hong Kong. Whether Hong Kong can maintain its multiple roles as a world metropolis and regional financial centre while becoming an essential part of China, depends a great deal on the mutual accommodations of the local born with these groups who eventually will take root in Hong Kong. Is this the last tango in Hong Kong?

When China says 'Mah zhao pao, wu zhao tiao' 'Keep on dancing, keep on horse racing' — a theme repeatedly taken up by the Beijing leaders and meant as reassurance — it grabs the imagination of only one part of Hong Kong's population. Material promises aside, for the local-born professionals, one question lingers: in the decade ahead, to what extent can 'the people of Hong Kong' choose to dance to their own tunes?' ❑

An edited version of 'Remade in Hong Kong: Cultural Identity and the Politics of Difference' a speech given in Hong Kong on 9 February 1996

*A Hong Kong native, **Professor Helen Fung-har Siu** joined the faculty of Yale University in 1982 and is currently a Professor of Anthropology and Chair of Yale University's Council on East Asian Studies. She is the author of several books and works on Chinese history, anthropology, and sociology, including* Down to Earth: The Territorial Bond in South China *(co-edited by David Faure, 1995)*

DANNY YUNG

Facing up

It was through my experience on the stage, plus more than 10 years and over 70 works with the *Twenty Faces* group I set up in the late 1970s, that I came into contact with every margin of Hong Kong society. From the early-1980s, almost every work encountered some form of rebuff. I discovered the Hong Kong establishment did not engage in dialogue, did not recognise the existence of margins and had no interest in developing an indigenous culture. Nevertheless, these rebuffs gave Hong Kong's marginal groups the chance to explore their relationship with the establishment and acquire a deeper insight into the contradictions between art and the establishment.

In theatre, the relationship between performers and audience, between director and company, mirrors the interplay between the mainstream and the marginal. In an open and progressive theatre, these relationships are a central theme constantly reworked to develop channels of communication, create mutual understanding and acceptance of different positions and roles. In this way, real dialogue can begin and creativity start to show through. Our experiences in the theatre can be put to use to resolve the cultural and historical problems that assail Hong Kong.

The relationship between the centre and its margins is subtle: seen from the centre, the margins can be regarded as opening up new territories, or as rebelling against the establishment. In the coming years, Hong Kong will not only be marginal on China's stage, but on the world stage too. If Hong Kong can use the stage to promote the particular strengths and experiences of the marginal, a dialogue can be established linking China and the rest of the world.

(Right) I copied the [furniture from] the visitor's reception room of the Great Hall of the People. Behind the leaders' chairs, two translators discuss differences between men, women and people in general, between the masses, the audience and the actors, between China, Taiwan and Hong Kong. In the course of translation the mood changes; the scene becomes an 'entertainment' with music. The leaders start teasing each other, sexual intercourse turns into wrestling, the stage turns into an execution ground. Words lose their meaning and the rules of the stage are newly defined... This script developed out of a work from 1983 with the same title which was the subject of an unprecedented banning by the Hong Kong government. After two years of negotiation and protest the government backed off.

(Right) In 1995, Hong Kong Urban Council wanted to censor this script at the last minute. However, thanks to the influence of the new political parties and media attention, their attempt failed. But it left its mark in the shape of a statement, read before each performance, to the effect that Hong Kong Urban Council took no responsibility for the contents of the play. The incident became a joke in Hong Kong's art world but it also reflected the exaggerated power struggle between the art world and the government at that time.

Two or three things you should know about Hong Kong
(1993/4/5)

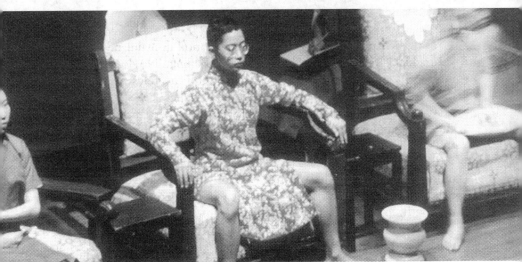

Chronicle of Women (1991)

Danny Yung *is a performance artist and the founder of Zuni Icosahedron, an art collective he founded in 1982*
Photos courtesy Zuni Icosahedron
Text translated by Jenny Putin; captions by Gerda Wielander

GEREMIE R BARMÉ

Hong Kong the floating city

Hong Kong has not only shaped much of China's popular culture, it has also been a key port for the packaging and re-export of Chinese dissident culture for over a decade. With its return to China in 1997, all that will come to an end. So, too, will its unique role in contemporary Chinese history as the mediator, mirror and filter for mainland and Taiwan exchanges

SINCE the early 1980s, the popular imagination in mainland China was gradually freed of the dominance of Beijing. No longer was the northern capital regarded as being the centre of the cultural universe and the sole source of social, political and cultural values. The stentorian tones of Central People's Broadcasting was replaced by a mellower register closer to that used in Taiwan's official media, and the rebirth of local radio and development of regional television helped to give the diverse peoples and cultures of the mainland a public voice and style of their own once more. The Beijing styles of dress — drab and ill-tailored revolutionary cotton and synthetic cloths — gave way to new paragons of fashion from the south, in particular Hong Kong.

The political charisma of Beijing had been in steady retreat ever since the fall of Lin Biao in 1971. This continued throughout the 1980s and was transformed into a form of revulsion following the student protests of 1989. The voice of the centre, of Beijing, was less a clarion call to revolution than a nagging reminder of the past and its outmoded political message. In terms of mass culture, 'the centre,' *zhongyang*, the focus of socio-political meaning in China — that body of symbols and associations that propped up a sense of identity, place and significance — now expanded to include Taiwan and Hong Kong.

The evolution of this 'Chinese commonwealth' began early with the clash between official disapproval and popular desire for Canto-pop music in the early 1980s. After numerous official bans and confiscations of cassette tapes, the works of massively popular singers like Taiwan's Teresa Teng (Deng Lijun, 1953-1995), Hou Dejian, Luo Dayou (Lo Ta-yu — now a leading media figure in Hong Kong) and the 'Four Heavenly Kings' (*sida tianwang*) of Hong Kong music, dominated teen culture on the mainland from the early 1990s.

The incursion from the south began with music, film theme songs and cinema; and it continued with cinema and a boom in literature (ranging from the romantic mush of Qiong Yao, Yi Shu and San Mao, to the martial arts novels of Jin Yong, Gu Long, Liang Yusheng, and Wen Ruian, as well as the 'cartoon classics' of the Hong Kong artist Cai Zhizhong). This new cultural impetus, the forerunner of the massive shift in mainland styles of expression, entertainment, consumption and self image, issued not from the West, but from 'Tai-Gang' as Hong Kong and Taiwan were spoken of in the shorthand of mainland officialese. In Hong Kong the Cantonese expression is Kong-Tai (Gang-Tai), in the order not of notional but empirical preference.

Fashions, hairstyles, consumer items, interior decorating, lifestyles, cuisine and even mainstream language increasingly began to emulate the south. As way stations, first Shenzhen and Zhuhai, the Special Economic Zones near Hong Kong, then Guangzhou, the capital of Guangdong Province, had also gained in prominence. Increasingly imitating Hong Kong (the local Cantonese long ago abandoned the strident revolutionary style of officialese for the softer, slick enunciation of the British territory), Guangzhou in the early 1990s was claimed by some to be the second most influential mainland city after Beijing. It has gone further than any other in sweeping away feudal remnants and introducing democratic elements to social life. Following the new wave of economic reforms of 1992, Shanghai began working hard to catch up.

Hong Kong had been importing new ideas into China for over a decade. It had also been the launching pad for the careers of China's much-vaunted new wave of film-makers including Cheng Kaige, Zhang Yimou, Tian Zhuangzhuang and Jiang Wen. It was through the enthusiasm of the young Hong Kong-born, but western-educated, organisers of the Hong Kong International Film Festival (people like

Leung Mou-ling, Lee Chok-to and Shu Kei) that the works of these
mainland directors and actors were first screened in Hong Kong and
introduced to the international film critics and film-festival organisers
who subsequently helped manufacture the Chinese film sensation
internationally. The same is true of the art world, for it was Johnson
Chang and David Tang of Shanghai Tang — and of The China Club,
Beijing's biggest, newest, brightest and most expensive club in the centre
of the heavenly city — who, with the aid of Beijing dissident art curators
and critics like Li Xianting, launched the post-1989 China avant-garde art
exhibitions that have become an international museum staple.

Mainland China's rock'n'roll culture was supported at crucial moments
in its history by contracts with Hong Kong music companies; these same
companies and entrepreneurs helped broker relations between the Beijing
singers and larger Taiwan companies.

IN HIS iconoclastic youth in the late 1970s and early 1980s, Luo Dayou
was famed around Taipei for dressing in black, sporting long hair and
wearing dark glasses, even at night. He presented a striking image to a
prim and proper society that was in many ways a clone of early 1960s US
culture. The lyrics of some of his songs mocked the Kuomintang (KMT)
authorities as well as fusty Confucian values, but it was as a romantic
singer that Luo became known on the mainland from 1983. Eventually,
small Luo Dayou fan clubs developed in Beijing and Shanghai.

Having moved to Hong Kong in 1988, in early 1991 Luo released a
song that directly addressed his concerns for the future of the territory,
now his adopted home. The porous nature of the audio-visual world of
greater China was demonstrated by the fact that within a short time of its
appearing in Hong Kong a copy of the MTV video tape of this pointedly
satirical song, 'Queen's Road East', was circulating among middle school
students in Beijing.

The video clip showed Luo and his collaborator, Lin Hsi, a Hong Kong
musician, dressed in Mao suits and dark glasses marching and singing in
the streets of Hong Kong's Central District as a group of Red Guards
struck various revolutionary poses in time with the music, or stood in line
waving bouquets of flowers to welcome the comrades from the north.
Some of the more choice lyrics, written by Lin, were as follows:

> There's this royal friend of mine, you find her on our coins
> She just never ages, and they all call her the Queen

Every time I go out shopping she comes along with me
Though her face doesn't show it, she's always a big hit
Our bosom friends go far away with only a 'bye-bye'
We'll have to rely on great comrades to try out their new ideas...

As the Hong Kong culture entrepot is called into question, so, too, will its unique role in contemporary Chinese history as the mediator for mainland and Taiwan exchanges. These have been numerous and complex. Although many contacts are direct these days, the cultural filter that Hong Kong has provided, in the media as in other realms, has been crucial in creating a larger China that has seen the wearing down of ideological differences and a more equitable relationship.

Cultural incursion is, however, a two-way street. While the year 1991 started out with Luo Dayou's light-hearted message of political gloom, it finished with an extraordinarily sophisticated and humorous MTV version of the Shenyang woman singer Ai Jing's song 'My 1997'. In the tones of a Chinese Suzanne Vega, the 22-year-old told of her rites of artistic passage from her home town in the northeast via Beijing where she had a stint in the East Song and Dance Ensemble led by the famous Wang Kun, to the Bund in Shanghai, eventually ending up in Guangzhou. Caught there she laments that her boyfriend, a Hong Kong

Chui Dian, Beijing 1990: one of the 'lucky ones';
Credit: Irene Slegt/Panos Pictures

resident (and music company executive who marketed Ai Jing and various Beijing rock'n'rollers), could freely travel to the mainland while she was not permitted to return the compliment. The lyrics of 'My 1997' perhaps reflect the wishes of other northern consumers as they survey the market and the pleasures of the south:

> Roll on 1997,
> Then I'll be able to go to Hong Kong!
> Roll on 1997,
> Let me stand in Hung Hom Stadium
> Roll on 1997,
> I can go with him to a midnight show!
> Come on, I want to find out
> What's so fragrant about the Fragrant Harbour.

At the end of one rendition of this song in Beijing, the singer added in sotto voce: 'Don't worry, only six more years to go.'

In November 1991, the Beijing-based non-official film maker Zhang Yuan completed a slick and humorous five-minute tape of Ai's song for MTV. It was played on Hong Kong television when the singer's first album was released there. And with a record-producer boyfriend in Hong Kong, it was not long before Ai Jing made her way to the territory to become part of the east-southeast Asian pop circuit.

The Hong Kong style with its hip, modernised Shanghai decadence — for it had inherited the traditions of China's only urbane international city after the fall of Shanghai in the late 1940s — worldly petit-bourgeois patina and consumer sheen, has profoundly shaped the face of mainland culture for the past 15 years. Writers and commentators on the mainland have had little chance to study the history of popular culture in Hong Kong and Taiwan; and cultural critics deprived of either the resources, or blinded by prejudice, have not given full weight to the significance of these formerly peripheral cultures. Similarly, the media has tended to concentrate on political and economic issues and not concerned itself with looking in the mirror of cultural life.

The commercial culture of Hong Kong and Taiwan — including advertising in both the electronic and print media — has a massive impact on the mainland. Kong-Tai has digested the global culture of Euro-America and Japan for 'Chinese' delectation and has developed a form of product presentation and placement that appeals directly to mainland consumers.

Yet the islands (Hong Kong and Taiwan) provide much more than this. For the cultural world of the mainland they are a source of off-shore funding and predigested cultural information, as well as being sites for exhibition and publication and a launching pad to the West — or at least the consumers of southeast Asia.

Despite their proximity to the mainland, people in Hong Kong are generally ignorant of the language, symbols, icons and fads of Chinese socialism. Nonetheless, attempts have been made to absorb mainland tropes as in the case of the music of Luo Dayou whose 1988 song 'Comrade Lover' (*Airen tongzhi*) contained lines like 'You're as beautiful as a slogan.' They are, nonetheless, ideological innocents and mainlanders deride them for it, although secretly jealous that they are forever deprived of the luxury of a relatively untroubled history. Unsullied by the horror and violence of Maoism, Hong Kong enjoys materialism, narrow social and national goals and pragmatism. These are prospects that both delight and unsettle people on the mainland.

H ONG KONG and Taiwan are, then, something of a 'missing link' for the mainland. In many areas, the significance of Kong-Tai culture has been that it has built on and developed the values of the New Culture and May Fourth Movements of the 1920s. Forced to eschew the radical leftism and utopianism that grew up in 1930s China (and which eventually won out on the mainland), the 'Kong-Tai-style' is more personal and intimate, more at home with the grand tradition of China while still engaged with the problems of modernity and westernisation. The 'Kong-Tai-style' allows space for the individual, as well as idiosyncrasy and irrelevance. While these things also concern mainland cultural figures, they are rarely of cultural usefulness to them per se. Ultimately, they are nugatory, barely more than minor distractions from major ideological debates and factional warfare.

But culture is not confined to these individuals, and perhaps the 'yuppie' style of Kong-Tai may lead the way for the small enclaves of cultivated wealth that are gradually appearing on the mainland. The classics of the West and the culture of Europe and America can be appreciated with relative equanimity by the educated of Taiwan, many of whom have studied or travelled overseas. There is also the ethos of a more broad-minded and worldly view that has its attractions for the new-rich of the mainland.

Kong-Tai provides them with models — both good and bad — they can emulate. The 1990s has seen the first efforts of Kong-Tai entrepreneurs to export or 're-port' this elite ambience to the mainland. Kong-Tai encountered and became absorbed into the cultural network before the mainland. As such, Kong-Tai-Chinese has developed a modern, fashionable and even post-modern vocabulary. It is a language that has provided the mainland media with a whole new style for speaking to its own people. Thus, the imports of Hong Kong, like those of Taiwan, have not merely been financial. There has also been an influence of style and possibilities, a glimpse of alternatives and otherness.

THE Hong Kong identity is not just that of the internationalised elite and its fin-de-siècle sophistication. There are strong elements of nationalism in the territory, and since the 1940s there has also been a pro-Communist substructure in the city. It has maintained a shadow existence, with primary and high schools, a publishing and media industry, business concerns and involvement with virtually every aspect of the territory's life. That influence has expanded in recent years.

As Hong Kong approaches its 'return to the bosom of the Motherland' (*huigui zuguode huaibao*) as the formula runs, elements of anti-western (imperialist, British and US) sentiment will come to the fore and be fostered by the mainland and Communist-connected Hong Kong media. There are also those among the outspoken individuals in favour of freedom who are also highly critical of how the British colonial administrators repeatedly stymied democratic reform in Hong Kong until it was too late. The patriotic significance of Hong Kong's return to the mainland is lost on no-one. It is part of the final process of what the Communist authorities, and many people in China, see as the reunification of a divided nation. First Hong Kong, then Macau (formally under Portuguese rule until 1999), and then, finally, Taiwan. ❏

Geremie R Barmé is a Senior Fellow in the Research School of Pacific and Asian Studies at the Australian National University, Canberra. His recent books include Shades of Mao: The Posthumous Cult of the Great Leader *(NY: M E Sharpe, 1996) and* In the Red, Contemporary Chinese Culture *(NY: Columbia University Press, forthcoming). He was an associate director of 'The Gate of Heavenly Peace' a three-hour historical documentary on the Chinese protest movement of 1989*

PENNY WROUT

Owners' options

The choice between free expression in their papers and the preservation of their business interests on the mainland presents proprietors with a dilemma. Or does it?

HONG KONG entrepreneurs can't believe their luck. They stand at the gateway to a market of over a billion souls and when the doors to China fly open on 1 July total access is theirs. On examination of the trends, media proprietors must be particularly excited. The introduction of market forces into Chinese socialism has had a prodigious effect on the appetite of readers. Since 1978 the number of newspapers available in China has shot up from 186 to 2,200 last year. There's been a similar growth in magazine titles, from 930 in 1978 to 8,100 in 1996.

Hong Kong also enjoys a thriving press with around 400 newspaper titles currently available. Many are owned by business people who have substantial interests in other sectors they would also like to see prosper in China. Robert Kuok for example, the Malaysian chairman of the *South China Morning Post*, was once known as the Sugar King of southeast Asia. He is one of the largest sugar traders within China, and has significant property and hotel investments there.

With such enormous potential just around the corner it would be a foolish proprietor indeed who ignored the pronouncements on media freedom emerging from Beijing. In 1995 China's vice-premier Qian Qichen spoke about the need for the colony's media to promote 'a loving China and Hong Kong spirit' on the basis of factual, ethical and responsible reporting. Taken at face value the comments appear reassuring. Seen in the Chinese context, words like factual, ethical and responsible take on a quite different meaning.

The Hong Kong media are responding to the mood of Chinese officials in a variety of ways. Some publications have stood fast by their criticisms of Beijing, notably the Chinese-language *Apple Daily*. That paper's reporters have paid the price by being consistently denied access to cover official events in mainland China. Its owner, Jimmy Lai, was forced to close down the Beijing branch of a separate retail business he controlled. Other firms are examining the feasibility of relocation, following a trend that has led to 60 per cent of Hong Kong-domiciled businesses registering elsewhere. Alternatively some editors have chosen to play along with the mood in Beijing, describing their policy as non-confrontational and realistic.

It's the policy of appeasement that worries the broader business community in Hong Kong most. They welcome the free flow of information and opinion that has made the territory southeast Asia's international media centre. So long as the world-wide news gatherers have bases in Hong Kong, companies have easy access to the international audience. If the news agencies were to detect a mood of intolerance or censorship and move elsewhere, confidence in Hong Kong as an open business centre would be badly undermined. A free press is seen as a kind of insurance policy against the corruption that continues to dog business ventures in China. Recent trends on the mainland have not been encouraging. At the beginning of 1996, foreign economic news services were put under the supervision of the New China News Agency, Xinhua, so Chinese organisations are unable to purchase economic information directly from foreign wire services.

IT WAS in this context that I interviewed a number of Hong Kong journalists working in different fields of the media and asked them about prospects for after 1997.

Stephen Vines has worked in Hong Kong since 1987. When the *South China Morning Post* was taken over by the pro-Beijing businessman Robert Kuok, he opened up a rival publication, the *Eastern Express*. His aim was to develop an English-language daily with no ties to China nor to Britain. By the time the paper folded in 1996, Vines had already left and has since worked as a freelance reporter, mainly for the *Independent* in London. He has detected a pragmatic line creeping into the colony's columns. 'People here are adjusting and preparing for 1997 and they understand fully that there won't be a free media so they're asking, "How do you position the media in Hong Kong so that it doesn't fall out of favour with the new masters and so it's possible to continue to flourish?".

Change of masters

Over the past decade, Hong Kong journalists have revelled in the opportunity to highlight the shortcomings of politicians and at times to poke fun at the Governor. Yet this latitude does not stretch back far enough to be considered a solid tradition of press freedom. Many journalists in Hong Kong remember a time when government interference was commonplace. Stephen Vines, a freelance journalist, speaks of an atmosphere of secrecy and control. 'The knee-jerk response of the colonial authority was to keep the media under wraps, not to give out information and to make life difficult for journalists who wanted to cover subjects the authorities didn't want covered.'

A shift in attitude started in the early 1980s with talks on the future of Hong Kong. As negotiations progressed, people demanded better information and the media responded with a more vigorous tone. Chris Patten's appointment and his much trumpeted commitment to democratic processes opened debate further, but Mak Yin Ting from the Hong Kong Journalists Association believes the British could have done more to foster free speech. When it comes to defending the rights of journalists, her association is toothless, since Hong Kong has no legislation permitting collective bargaining, no trade unions and lots of draconian legislation still on the statute book.

Observers of the Hong Kong media note that even before the 1980s the British rein on the Chinese-language press was looser than on its English counterpart — largely because most officials were unable to read Cantonese. That marks out the *South China Morning Post* — seen as the English-language paper of record — as the publication most noted for its editorial turnaround. The man currently in charge there, Jonathan Fenby, freely acknowledges that five or 10 years ago, 'It would have been a paper that was very much the colonial mouthpiece, whose editor would go to tea with the Governor once or twice a week and come back and write those editorials. We're much more independent now.' Critics of the paper say that since Robert Kuok took over in 1993 the paper has simply swapped masters.

Fenby insists that the paper is and will remain committed to the western ideal of a free press, though he concedes his publication is unlikely to find it plain sailing after 1997. Much will depend, he says, on 'whether we continue to operate just in the goldfish bowl reporting on Hong Kong, or if we are seen in a wider Chinese context'. In other words, he can expect more interference from Chinese authorities if the paper is viewed as a pan-China publication. *PW*

The consequence is that you get not so much the misreporting of events, as the non-reporting of events. So, for example, Hong Kong's biggest political party, the Democratic Party, gets markedly less coverage than the largest party would in any other free society. You don't see much about what's going on in Tibet. You don't see much about levels of corruption in China, and I must stress that you used to.'

Vines has made it his business to speak to all the international news agencies in Hong Kong and three of the broadcasting organisations. He says that practically every international newsgathering organisation with its Asian base in Hong Kong has been looking at alternative locations, but none are prepared to go on the record about their contingency plans. 'The ease with which you can re-hook up computers is such that if push comes to shove they can move very quickly indeed. If, for example, all journalists have to be licensed to operate in Hong Kong, as they do in China, these organisations will move at very short notice.' Lee Kuan Yew, the former prime minister of Singapore has been in Hong Kong to promote his country as an alternative media centre.

IF you take a cab in Hong Kong between nine o'clock and mid-day, the chances are you will also be listening to Albert Cheng's show *Teacup in a Storm* on Commercial Radio. The news-based comment programme is modelled on a television show he co-hosted on Hong Kong's Home Channel in 1994. *Newstease* ran for 52 editions and achieved some of the highest audiences the territory has ever mustered. 'We broke the tradition in Hong Kong which used to be humble and complimentary. We brought TV confrontation on air; this was a pioneering show.'

Despite the audience figures *Newstease* was dropped, Albert Cheng believes, because it offended pro-China politicians, though the Channel bosses at ATV never admitted as much. 'They said they were rescheduling and paid us a retainer saying, "We'll bring you back after three months," but we knew that would never come, so we enjoyed getting paid for three months then that was it. They were trying to shut us up, not to talk about the problems.' Cheng has held onto his daily outlet on radio but thinks the atmosphere for broadcasters in Hong Kong has deteriorated. 'When Chris Patten came to Hong Kong, he started promoting democracy and fighting with China. It was unspoken, but the Hong Kong government started to encourage people to express their opinions, and that's why the atmosphere opened up in TV and radio. The government relaxed the enforcement of various controls so the climate was quite open, but the closer we get to 1997, Mr Patten himself has shut up and I guess the media owners go with the trend and become more cautious.'

THE Hong Kong Journalists Association is concerned about the trend. In conversations with members, Mak Yin Ting, the association's chairwoman, is constantly having to urge journalists not to succumb to self-censorship in their coverage of China. 'Some of my colleagues say, "Oh no, I can't run with that because the editor will put it straight in the rubbish bin" so they just drop the idea. I tell them that they shouldn't restrain themselves if they judge it newsworthy.' She and others on the association's executive stress the importance of maintaining the tradition of free speech: 'I do not know how much we'll lose if we stand firm, but I can say if we give up first we'll lose everything.'

That gloomy tone is counterbalanced by Mak Yin Ting's observations of Chinese journalists operating in Beijing. For 10 years she's been on periodic trips to China on behalf of Radio Hong Kong and lately, she says, as more reporters from Hong Kong have brought their working practices to the mainland, Chinese journalists have begun to seek out their own story. 'In the past the reporters would just wait for their assignment from their editor. If there was something they didn't know they wouldn't ask, but recently our ways of working have stimulated them. Even in the National People's Congress they'll ask the officials questions, just like us. That was unimaginable five years ago. So with more chance to work together I hope the gap will close.'

IT'S an optimistic tone that is echoed by Loh Chan from *Apple Daily*. He is the publisher of Hong Kong's second most popular paper, established as recently as 1995 to provide a voice for the full range of political opinion and still stridently independent of China. 'If "one country, two systems" is going to work then it needs monitoring and it needs feedback from all the people of Hong Kong. We are quite confident. After all, why should China rock the boat? We don't have any contingency plan and how could we? We're a local paper for Hong Kong and if we move away we don't exist. Entering 1997 we're going to have a two to three year honeymoon period. After that it depends on economic and political developments, the environment of competition among the Asian countries and on China's relations with Taiwan, because we're going to be a showroom for Taiwan.'

If *Apple Daily* is the new kid on Hong Kong's media block, the English language *South China Morning Post*, established at the beginning of the century, is one of its foundation stones (see p163). The editor, Jonathan Fenby, has been in place since May 1995. Many ex-pat journalists accuse him of bowing to pressure from his proprietor Robert Kuok to go gently on China. He fiercely denies any proprietorial interference but foresees a culture clash with the Chinese authorities after 30 June. 'You've got a very big problem there. How do you maintain a free approach to journalism when you are part of a country that has a completely different view of what the media is and sees it as part of the power apparatus? I think you should try to explain to the Chinese authorities how the press works here. A few months ago, I wrote a long leading article about the importance of press freedom and I was criticised here, including by Government House who thought the leader wasn't sufficiently thunderous. But what that article was trying to do was to explain what a free press is, why it's important and why it's an element in the current success of Hong Kong. But of course when you do that here, you're immediately seen as having compromised with the censor. The point is to try and influence the censor rather than saying "publish and be damned", because you may well be damned.'

All these journalists believe that the fate of the media after handover will be a strong indicator of how far China will want to interfere with other aspects of Hong Kong's economy and political structure. That puts them in an uncomfortable position. They are both reporters and leading actors in the events that will shape Hong Kong in the next century. ❏

Penny Wrout *is a BBC radio and TV reporter*

LARRY FEIGN

The world of Lily Wong

'The World of Lily Wong', 18 May 1995. Self-fulfilling prophecy?
This cartoon won first place in the Amnesty International Human Rights Press Award

'The World of Lily Wong', 19 May 1995.
That evening 'The World of Lily Wong' was terminated with immediate effect

Larry Feign *is a cartoonist and creator of 'The World of Lily Wong', a much loved feature in the* South China Morning Post. *It was terminated in 1995*

For more of Larry Feign's cartoons see his World Wide Web site: http://www.asiaonline.net/lilywong.
For more banned cartoons see http://www.pond.com/wittyworld/censorship/, and http://www.oneworld.org/index_oc/

INTERVIEW

HUANG YUMIN

Mad dog tipster

At one time a professor in the department of current affairs at Zhuhai University, Huang Yumin is now in charge of Current Affairs on Hong Kong commercial radio and HK Television. In March 1996 he set up *Dian Gou Daily* (Mad Dog), a newspaper devoted to pungent political comment. He was interviewed by Yang Lian in October 1996

What was the point in setting up Dian Gou Daily *with 1997 so near?*

Huang Yumin In Hong Kong I am a critic and a commentator. My newspaper positions itself alongside the interests of ordinary Hong Kong people and confronts the political authorities. That includes the Chinese government, the government of Hong Kong and other political parties and factions. I emphasise independence not neutrality; sedulous neutrality in our situation would be meaningless. To criticise is certainly to destroy. To rebuild is the responsibility of those being criticised — the authorities.

We have taken the name *Dian Gou* in the sense of a watch dog for Hong Kong society. The news media are society's watch dog, monitoring political power and politics.

HUANG YUMIN

Hong Kong is a commercial society, is your newspaper going to be able to survive?

IT is primarily critical of the government, but it also carries daily analysis on the horse racing scene. This ensures that the readership is kept broad and increases the ability of the paper to survive and have influence. Other newspapers publish 50-60 pages daily and so have to rely on advertising revenue. I publish a two-sheet format [equally divided between comment and the hot tips from the track] and can survive on sales revenue alone. As it's the horse racing season at the moment we can publish and sell more than 10,000 copies. If other factors don't interfere, stepping over and beyond 1997 ought to be no problem.

By 'other factors' you mean political interference. Are you an optimist?

AT present, the Hong Kong news media are withdrawing and demarcating the 'bottom line' entirely of their own volition. To make money and to survive, the are preparing for post-1997 by offering more economic news with less comment on society and none at all on politics. But I take the position that to stand still is to lose ground, so I aim to strike forward and break through their bottom line. If, after 1997, they want to close this paper, then they will have to pass some despicable laws. This would have implications for freedom of speech for the whole of Hong Kong. I am only too happy to provide a test case. If *Dian Gou* is censored then freedom of speech is empty talk. Let the future government of the Hong Kong Special Administrative Region have its test case: if even *Dian Gou* can survive, then freedom of speech is a reality.

If they are afraid that the other mass media will unite behind you, they would doubtless be glad to see you closed down as soon as possible. What would you do?

FOR the first few years after Hong Kong is returned I don't think the situation will be that bad overall. I intend to use this time to carve out a space — a space during which *Dian Gou* survives in a climate of freedom of speech that can be used to maximum effect in influencing public opinion and encouraging independent thought. Even if the situation deteriorates, what would have been the point of doing nothing? I could lay my pen aside but I cannot twist, distort or surrender. I could refrain from writing and keep quiet, but I am incapable of writing or speaking against my conscience.

Over the last 50 years, Hong Kong has acted as a political and economic conduit and a centre for cultural information for the mainland, Taiwan and southeast Asia. Can it sustain this after 1997?

BASICALLY yes. Take the mainland for example. Wang Dan is about to be sentenced [*Wang Dan was sentenced to 11 years in prison on 30 October*], and yet for quite some time he has been able to have links with the outside world. This is due to today's global information technology. Unless it abandons Hong Kong's market economy, the Communist Party cannot ban news and information. On the mainland Internet access and fax machines are now very common. The authorities have no way of constantly checking what is being sent and received. If they want to protect Hong Kong's economic well-being, then they have to protect its means of communication with the outside world.

This sounds very optimistic. Is the Communist Party that concerned with Hong Kong's economy?

THERE are still differences between Hong Kong and the mainland. The mainland news media are nearly all publicly-owned, whilst Hong Kong's are, for the most part, private. This is not to be unduly optimistic, but we cannot just stand by; we have to try and achieve something. At the same time, the mainland itself is in a state of change, it cannot even assure its own 'stability and unity'. As for probing the bottom line, Hong Kong's people are highly pragmatic and more than capable of exploiting any loophole open to them.

So what is your definition of 'Chinese People'?

IT has to be based on history and culture. A kind of moral imperative and a cultural awareness. The moral imperative is due to our blood ties. As a Chinese one should hope for an (even bad) Chinese government that culturally is based on the points of difference from western and other cultures. I defend nationalism, but not the nationalism that the Communist Party manipulates to squeeze democracy, or used during the Japanese War of Resistance against the Kuomintang, or that, after 1949, has been used against dissidents. The Communist Party has never been 'nationalist' or even 'internationalist' but purely totalitarian. This regime remains unrepentant just because the Chinese people are far too tolerant.

You talk of 'national' cultural awareness. As a cultured Hong Konger, how do you define 'Hong Kong culture'?

HONG Kong is a meeting place between Chinese and western cultures. We can think independently, go abroad to study and have easy access to books published on the mainland, in Taiwan or in the West. Hong Kong's point of difference is that it tends towards diversity. As a result, the people of Hong Kong have developed more mixed cultural values.

One set of values cannot be replaced easily by another. There is no single ideology that could ever become over-dominant in Hong Kong such as the 'Three Principles of the People' in Taiwan or Communism on the mainland. The downside of such a society is a weakened ability to unite. The benefit is that such a society embraces many shades of opinion and is able to judge between right and wrong.

Of course there is a much greater concentration of Chinese people in Hong Kong than in other places overseas and so it must in itself represent a kind of Chinese culture.

After 1997, Hong Kong's diverse culture will lose the British democratic guarantee. There will be an unaccustomed environment of self-reliance. What does this imply for the intellectual community? Do you really believe in '50 years without change'?

THE most fundamental change will certainly be political and to do with freedom of speech. Nobody in Hong Kong believes in 'no change for 50 years'. Most people are watching; quietly waiting for change.

I often say to intellectuals and to other people: 'If you do not weep before you are confronted with your coffin it's a bit late when you are already being lowered in.' So this really is the time for Hong Kong people to hang on to their 'self', to stand up for this climate of cultural diversity if they want it to continue.

In 1979 everyone was hailing Deng Xiaoping as the great emancipator. Wei Jingsheng declared 'there are no Four Modernisations without democratisation' and was sentenced to 15-years' imprisonment for treason. On his release he continued to maintain and participate in the Democracy Movement and was condemned last year to a further 14-years' imprisonment for subversion. Hong Kong's Basic Law lists the crimes of 'subversion', 'splittism' and so on — a future place in the dock for the Wei Jingshengs of Hong Kong. Are you not afraid of becoming Hong Kong's Wei Jingsheng?

ARTICLE 23 of Hong Kong's Basic Law enumerates crimes such as 'subverting the central people's government', 'splitting the motherland' and 'stealing state secrets'. After 1997, what will be considered 'subversion', 'splittism', what are 'state secrets'? Where is the benchmark to judge these things?

We pointed these things out early on. Since then, Wang Xizhe has come to Hong Kong [and moved on to the USA], Wang Dan has been sentenced and Liu Xiaobo sent for labour reform. These strike hard at the heart of the Hong Kong people. This logic of Party = State, opposition = treason is the greatest threat to Hong Kong's people.

Internationally the Chinese government is playing the economic card as well as the political card, playing off different countries and corporations with the promise of import and export contracts, joint ventures and investment in China in an attempt to reduce western pressure on human rights in China. Can this strategy succeed?

NOT really. The Chinese government always insists that the Chinese market is ever-growing, that the investment climate is ever better and that future profits are ever higher. But none of these things are proven. Western business functions on a system and does not blindly believe boasting and unsubstantiated conjecture. Hard evidence is required, including media scrutiny. 'If America gets belligerent then we will pass our money over to the British, who will toe the line.' Such a subjective, do-as-we-please, governmental approach is not good enough.

The West should understand the workings of Chinese mainland politics and the realities of the economic situation thoroughly, not just subjectively hope or speculate in the light of its own value systems or look for gain. As for Hong Kong, it should not seek to find in the troubles of the transfer of sovereignty affirmations of its own past political successes. Britain in particular has a moral responsibility to make its position clear when Hong Kong is succumbing to mainland Communist pressure and not act as a bystander. ❏

Translated by Simon Kirby

The first to go

Credit: *Rhodri Jones/Panos Pictures*

THE world's major newspapers, TV stations and news agencies booked their suites in Hong Kong's top hotels for the night of 30 June 1997 long ago: it's the last great photo-opportunity of the twentieth century. And when the curtain finally rises on this carnival — for which the date has long been set, the publicity long distributed, the audience long waiting on the edge of their seats — what drama will be played out?

The banks will be working, the shops will be open as usual, the ferries will be running, the street stalls will still be selling their fragrant delicacies. Nothing will have happened. There will be no 'red ocean' as in the Cultural Revolution, nor tanks on the streets as in Beijing on 4 June 1989. No secret policemen in evidence clutching lists, tracking down counter-revolutionaries; the 9,000 or so troops of the People's Liberation Army will be safely behind the walls of their barracks. There'll be none of the images of Communism the West is expecting. Just a flag, which would have been flying anyway, now fluttering alone in the silence.

And should you take a short stroll from downtown Kowloon to the Star Ferry, you probably won't notice that, among the brightly coloured Chinese titles and the smiles of the girls on the cover of *Penthouse* and *Playboy,* a few magazines will have disappeared from the news-stands.

Western correspondents, their minds still filled with images of the live horror movie that was the Tiananmen Massacre, probably won't notice either: a few magazines specialising in political comment — which never sold particularly well in the first place — have stopped publication. What's so odd about that? If anything serious had happened, the Hong Kong people, nurtured on the milk of western democracy, would certainly speak out. But this time there will be no demonstrations, no protests, slogans nor tears. These are no longer 'Hong Kong people', they're not even simply 'Chinese'; they are learning how to be 'People's Republic Chinese' — learning to be silent.

Hong Kong's independent voices, the voices that so recently protested the resentencing of Wei Jingsheng, the imprisonment of Wang Dan and Liu Xiaobo, that condemned the massacre and arrests in Tiananmen, that for half a century have held the Communist government to account, will have disappeared. Those publications which cannot, don't want to, or at least haven't yet changed direction, will be the first to go in post-July Hong Kong.

Index asked the editors of some of these to talk about their personal expectations and the future of their papers.

Yang Lian

JIN ZHONG
Turned back at the border

Jin Zhong of Open Magazine

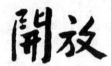
IN March 1996, on my way to Shenzhen to visit a niece who had gone to Guangdong for her honeymoon, I was detained, gifts in hand, for one and a half hours at Chinese Customs. Having examined the computer records, a public security officer escorted me back to the border where I was informed, 'Your visitor's permit has been confiscated. We do not welcome your return. Have a nice Spring Festival!'

I left China for Hong Kong in 1980 but have returned frequently, even visiting prominent people in Beijing. Suddenly, I had become an undesirable, 'entry refused'.

I was born in China and my nationality is Chinese. I am a Hong Kong resident with 'permanent residence' status; have never sought a US passport; have not violated Chinese laws. Yet I have been deprived of my right to return. This is indeed sorrowful.

I am, of course, well aware why they didn't want me back in China: I edit a magazine they don't much like. In my 16 years in Hong Kong, this is all I have done, edit my magazine and write my articles.

I belong to the generation that witnessed the disastrous policies of Mao Zedong. Well before the start of the Cultural Revolution, we were aware of his crimes and lived for the day we could expose them. Our criticism of the Communist regime, including Deng Xiaoping, is tantamount to criticism of Mao. But if Mao's monstrous legacy cannot be surmounted, modernisation will not succeed.

Commercial tides are surging forward over the Divine Land, yet the government continues to deprive its people of information and inflict its citizens with loss of memory. Any overstepping of the bounds is severely dealt with: Wei Jingsheng, first sentenced to 15 years for his articles, has been imprisoned again for a further 14 years. What can we say when a country ruled by the all-powerful dictatorship of the proletariat is mortally afraid of a single dissident voice?

Compared with Wei Jingsheng, we overseas dissidents are lucky. We may agonise over market pressures and the survival of our papers, but we do not fear the sound of footsteps on the stairs, the knock at the door.

On my way back from the Shenzhen border, it suddenly dawned on me: a country that imposed

a 14-year jail sentence for a single article couldn't possibly tolerate the likes of me; I must have written thousands in my time. I had to laugh. ❑

Jin Zhong is the editor of Open Magazine

Translated by Associated Translators, London

LEE YEE

Stick to the facts

九十年代 SINCE the Chinese Communist Party came to power in 1949, high level politics have been conducted behind closed doors, and ordinary people kept in ignorance of the facts. For more than 40 years, news about the People's Republic has mostly been spread via the press in Hong Kong; frequently, it is only through the re-circulation of such stories back into China that people there learn what is going on in their own country. This has had a significant influence on political developments there.

Despite lapses, the Hong Kong press has, over the past 40 years, by and large got it right — to which Beijing usually attests some time after the event and despite its accusations of 'rumour-mongering' or 'maliciously attacking China's leaders'. Political differences apart, commentators here have usually been on the side of the Chinese people against Party.

Given the patchy and politically motivated economic data from China, foreign investors have also come to rely on the financial information emanating from Hong Kong. Since China 'opened its doors' in 1978, the Hong Kong press has by and large encouraged foreign investment in China. Freedom of speech is essential to Hong Kong's role as an international financial centre.

I have worked in Hong Kong media circles for a number of decades. Despite the twists and turns, I still value the freedom of speech that has resulted from British rule. In Hong Kong ideas collide, people exchange opinions freely: an intellectual can speak his mind on subjects forbidden in China without endangering his personal safety.

However, in the run-up to 1997, the colours of press freedom are starting to fade. Beijing's conservative leaders intend to maintain a secure grip on public opinion in Hong Kong by imposing the potentially agonising 'one state, two systems' formula. This is aimed at dealing first with the gradually increasing calls for democracy among the people of Hong Kong, and then with the freedoms of speech and the press they already enjoy.

The twenty-third article of the Basic Law of the Hong Kong Special

Suitable cases for treatment

The Communist Party of China regards Hong Kong's media as a kind of assault weapon trained on China's peaceful evolution. It retaliates by a war of attrition against the territory's 'reactionary press', the so-called 'blacklist'.

Ways of punishing this recalcitrant bunch include: prohibiting their publication and circulation in mainland China; prohibiting Chinese-funded companies and organisations from advertising in them or providing any financial support; prohibiting their editors and reporters from gathering news and conducting interviews in mainland China; restricting assistance to left-wing printing and distributing organisations; vilifying their publishers, editors and reporters.

The following appear to have qualified for treatment:

Cheng Ming, monthly first published 1977, edited by Wen Hui. Frequently attacked by China for 'rumour mongering'. Not optimistic about the post-July situation.

Trend, sister monthly of *Cheng Ming*.

The Nineties, monthly first published 1970, edited by Lee Yee. Pessimistic about the future, says its 'focus will be shifting to Taiwan'.

Open Magazine, monthly first published 1987, edited by Jin Zhong. Says it will continue to publish in Hong Kong after 1997.

Front-Line Magazine, monthly first published 1991, edited by Liu Dawen. Says it will continue to publish after 1997.

China Spring, monthly published from the USA edited by Xu Bangtai.

Beijing Spring, monthly, similar to *China Spring*, edited by Yu Dahai.

Hong Kong Economic Journal, first published 1973 by Lam Shan-Muk.

Next, weekly first published 1990, focused on entertainment and owned by Jimmy Lai. Any political content merely decorative.

Apple Daily, first published 1995, owned by Jimmy Lai.

Mad Dog Daily, first published in spring 1996 by Huang Yumin. Has adopted clear-cut anti-Communist tone.

Ming Pao, first published 1959, frequently criticised by China. *JZ*

Translated by Associated Translators, London

> *Zunzi is a cartoonist.*
> *Many of his cartoons have been banned in the mainland...*
>
> **'1997 is a sensitive year for all of us. I'll stay in Hong Kong and do my best to carry on business as usual. Sure we'll defend our freedom of expression whenever it's at risk. The newspapers I'm drawing for are on the 'liberal' side, so I don't think I'll lose my 'battle ground' overnight'**

Region stipulates legislation to ban 'inciting the people to rise in rebellion'. In May and August 1996, Lu Ping, State Council minister responsible for Hong Kong and Macao, twice clarified that, after 1997, the Hong Kong press would under no circumstances be able to 'advocate' 'two Chinas', 'China and Taiwan as separate states' or 'independence for Hong Kong and Taiwan'. In October, Qian Qichen, China's vice-premier and foreign secretary, indicated that after 1997, the Hong Kong press would not be able to spread 'rumours or lies' or 'make personal attacks on leaders of the Chinese government'.

The Nineties, which reports mainly on the political situation on either side of the Taiwan Straits, will be unable to continue its current policy of independent opinion after 1997. It's somewhat alarming that though Lu Ping delivered his warning against 'advocating' 'two Chinas' at a press conference in Hong Kong, yet not one of those present raised any objection. Self-censorship has begun — and will become even more evident after 1997.

The Nineties will not engage in self-censorship. Nor will it adjust its editorial policy to conform to a political climate dictated by China. We know that Hong Kong cannot enjoy prosperity or stability without freedom of the press. We intend to remain in Hong Kong and strive for as large an arena for free expression as possible. We also intend to put out a Taiwanese edition of the journal, just in case we find ourselves unable to continue in Hong Kong. ❏

Lee Yee is the editor of The Nineties *magazine*

Translated by Desmond Skeel

MING LEI

Staying on

 ALTHOUGH a few of our wealthiest, pro-Chinese businessmen hail Hong Kong's 'better future' under Chinese rule, for most people, especially those in the media, July 1997 looks more like a nightmare: history's joke for the millennium.

Already officials like Qian Qichen, China's vice-premier and foreign minister, are cautioning us on what may and may not be said: 'They can put forward criticism, but not rumours or lies. Nor can they put forward personal attacks on the Chinese leaders. For that would not live up to the morality of the occupation. And that is not compatible with personal moral ethics as well.'

Cheng Ming, the most popular political magazine in Hong Kong and among overseas Chinese, will be the first of its kind to be subjected to enormous political pressures before and after July 1997. Letters, faxes and telephone calls from readers in more than 100 countries express the same anxiety: will *Cheng Ming* continue to exist unchanged after July 1997?

In our editorial marking the magazine's nineteenth anniversary, we gave our readers the following reply:

'Wherever you are, we have but one reply to you: we will continue to publish as usual. This is no more than our duty. Harassment and tyranny do not have unlimited power. We know that the claws of the tyrant will stretch out to us when it suits him, but he will be confronted by the masses of our readers and contributors across the world. We are not alone! Along with our supporters, we have decided to defend and fight for freedom of expression and democratisation in Hong Kong and China.' ❏

Ming Lei is executive editor of Cheng Ming

LIU DAWEN

Ever the optimist

Liu Dawen of Front-Line magazine

PERHAPS because my experience is so different, I am not entirely pessimistic about the future of free expression in Hong Kong — or even in the People's Republic of China come to that.

For nearly 30 years, I lived at the lowest level of Chinese society in the countryside. As a result, I feel deeply about the hardships visited on the nation and the people by the havoc of Communist rule. Conversely, I have experienced at much closer hand than most the progress made under the 'open door policy'.

Progress is painfully slow and tortuous but it will not stagnate. The last-ditch struggle of reactionary forces is facing defeat: they are not as powerful as they seem. In the Han areas, the Party is arresting fewer and fewer political prisoners. On any street corner people can discuss and even rebuke the leaders of the Party without it being considered a crime. People can move freely within China and even go abroad. Government bodies from the county-level down have conducted rudimentary democratic elections. These are all unprecedented achievements.

The imprisonment of Wei Jingsheng, Liu Xiaobo and Wang Dan is a temporary setback. The ideas of people like Wei Jingsheng and their supporters has touched a raw nerve in the Party. Its reaction is that of someone plunging unprepared into an unexploded minefield with all the risks that entails.

However, the vast majority of Chinese are content to go along with the Party's 'peaceful evolution', gradually chiselling away at the foundations of Communist Party rule. The Party has tossed aside any remaining pretentions to Marxism-Leninism: what remains of Chinese 'socialism' is nothing more than a facade. The transformation of the proletarian vanguard into the bourgeoisie is all but complete. All that remains is for the Party either to collapse or transform itself from within.

We should not be pessimistic about Hong Kong's future. In the short term, the road ahead will be bumpy: caught between the present 'Beijing factor' and the desperate opposition of those who consider themselves cornered, freedom of speech and freedom of the press will, to a degree,

remain under threat. In the longer term, the Party cannot stem the 'raging tide' of democracy indefinitely either in Hong Kong or in the People's Republic. When things reach a certain pitch, the pendulum must swing back in the opposite direction. For decades the people have lived in terror; now it is the rulers who tremble in the face of the tide of 'peaceful evolution'. ❏

Liu Dawen is the editor of Front-Line *magazine*

Translated by Desmond Skeel

LO FU

Baffled

'PEOPLE in their twenties who do not believe in Communism are useless. People in their forties who still believe in Communism are equally useless.' I first heard these words of George Bernard Shaw half a century ago. Now I am over 70, the end of the century is near and I have no idea whether or not my life has been of the slightest use.

In my twenties, I decided to devote my life to publicity work for the revolution. During World War II, in the year that the Pacific war broke out [1941], I joined the newspaper *Ta Kung Pao* in my home town of Guilin, a place eulogised by the poets as 'the supreme landscape of the Universe'.

I worked for the Party and its policies through its underground newspapers and magazines, but I did not become a member until 1948, after I arrived in Hong Kong and under pressure from my more radical friends. Why didn't I take the initiative myself? Because as a libertarian, I was unwilling to lose too much of my freedom to the Party. Indeed, throughout my 34 years of membership, I remained in doubt about class warfare and the dictatorship of the proletariat.

In 1983 it was announced in Beijing that I was being expelled. I was convicted as an 'American spy' and sentenced to 10 years' imprisonment, immediately commuted to probation and confinement to Beijing.

Things like the 'land reformation' murdered a lot of innocents. 'Against the rightists' destroyed even more intellectual lives. The 'great leap forward' was, in theory, a 'fight against heaven and earth' but it fought humanity on a grand scale. It also destroyed village productivity and led to the 'three years of adversity'. The 'Cultural Revolution' brought even more suffering in its train. The 'three-year' and '10-year' plans brought thousands of deaths through torture and starvation. In all, the death toll is more than all the slaughter in the eight-year Sino-Japanese war.

A decade of reform and openness has turned the tide from class warfare to economic growth, but there are still those in Beijing who would turn back the tide.

Throughout my years in the Party, I encountered the profound ignorance of my comrades. Their ignorance was a reflection of that within the secrecy-ridden Party hierarchy itself. As tools of the Party's policy of pacifying the population at large — and following Mao's much quoted version of an ancient adage: 'Confuse the people to help the people understand' — their 'politics of idiocy' succeeded only in spreading a culture of ignorance throughout the country. Most of us got used to being the tools of the 'idiocy policy'. Since independent thought was taboo, how could we exercise any influence?

Bit by bit, the eyes of this responsible Communist publicist were opened. The death of Lin Biao, the collapse of Jiang Qing, were shocks that awoke the nation. But what finally woke me where my 10-year imprisonment failed, was that during my detention in Beijing I personally witnessed the 1989 student democracy movement; heard with my own ears the guns and tanks of 4 June.

There was no place left for self-delusion. The 'Soviet Empire' had collapsed. What hope now for the Communist International? I felt relief that I was no longer a Party member. I also felt baffled by my entire life.

Yet I have no regrets. The Chinese Communist Party was a genuine revolutionary movement, corrupt only in middle age. Would that the Party could regain its youth. ❏

Lo Fu came to Hong Kong with Ta Kung Pao *in 1948. Today he is an independent writer and journalist*

Translated by Chiao-ling Chang

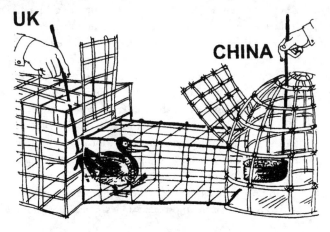

CHARLES GODDARD

Breathing space

For two decades or more, Hong Kong was the primary source of information for China-watchers of all kinds: the lung that drew in information from the mainland — and often spirited it back in the opposite direction.

This was never more crucial than in the 1960s and 1970s, particularly during the turbulent years of the Cultural Revolution. An isolationist China was a China the world was at pains to understand. Considerable resources were devoted to this end. The US consulate in Hong Kong bulged with intelligence operatives sifting and analysing each and every snippet of information that stole across the border. And like their US counterparts, British intelligence too had its own listening post monitoring mainland radio broadcasts and military communications.

Academics or journalists were equally well served, either by the University Services Centre with its seminal collection of mainland newspapers and periodicals, or by the Jesuits who published *China News Analysis*, a dry but detailed bulletin on political, economic and social developments in China. Even more important was the constant monitoring of human rights, including the fluctuating state of free expression.

With the arrival of China's open door policy during the 1980s, organisations specialising in monitoring a closed China went into quiet decline. But it would be a mistake to believe Hong Kong's role has been entirely eclipsed. True, it is no longer the primary source of information on China it once was, even on business and economic information. Yet with its more relaxed environment for publishing and for freedom of expression generally, the city colony remains a centre for numerous publications and information services — local, regional and international — specialising in information that mainland authorities consider politically sensitive, information which by its very nature is difficult to address openly within China, much less obtain, publish or disseminate. News about mainland human rights abuses and dissidents is a critical case in point. Even in these last months before the handover to Chinese sovereignty, Hong Kong is still the first port of call for dissidents escaping persecution in China. The affinity of language and culture, its geographical proximity, the perception (albeit diminishing) that Hong Kong is the most accessible safe haven, that it is a conduit to a more open world beyond China, are powerful magnets for those harassed or pursued by the Chinese authorities.

Something similar might be said for those whose freedom of expression is frustrated. Hong Kong's small coterie of China-watching publications, among them *The Nineties* and *Open Magazine*, publish pseudonymous articles from mainlanders, or carry reports citing classified documents or internal sources. These publications are among those few in Hong Kong which the Chinese authorities seek to 'isolate and attack' as part of a united front strategy — adopted with some success since the Beijing massacre in June 1989 — to co-opt or neutralise the local media in the run-up to the handover.

The mainstream media can also fall foul of Beijing over their China coverage. Those at greatest risk are journalists working the mainland beat who transgress China's strict parameters of information gathering. Leung Wai-man, a reporter with Hong Kong's *Express Daily News*, was detained in Beijing in October 1992 for having received a copy of a speech to be made by party leader Jiang Zemin. Though she was later released, her alleged accomplice, Wu Shishen, an editor in the domestic section of the Xinhua News Agency, was given a life sentence. More visible, perhaps, was the case of Hong Kong-based journalist Xi Yang who, in March 1994, was handed a 12-year prison sentence for 'stealing state financial secrets' — among them, unpublished interest rate changes. The prosecution was perceived in Hong Kong as a blunt message to the local media of the boundaries of acceptable journalism in China.

China understands, of course, that it cannot restrict freedom of expression and information in Hong Kong as it does on the mainland. But there will be less room for manoeuvre where there are issues of greater sensitivity at stake; less space for those whom Beijing has singled out to 'isolate and attack', those who will not join the consensus. The oxygen will be cut off, slowly, perhaps imperceptibly at first for some, more sharply for others. But there will still be space at the edges to breathe, even if less easily than before.

Charles Goddard *is a film maker and member of the Hong Kong Journalists Association*

HUANG YONGYU

Animal antics

BEFORE the earthquake in Xingtai in 1964, I was working in the Four Clean-ups Movement in a local production brigade. Whenever I was at a loose end, I made notes on animals and, before long, had a collection of 80 or so. They amused my colleagues, so I decided to illustrate them and get them published when I got back to Beijing.

We returned to the capital with the start of the Cultural Revolution. There were more than 1,000 of us — writers and artists — stationed in the western suburbs. Living conditions were fine, but tension was high. After a month or so, we were sent back to our colleges to take part in the huge struggle meetings.

Next day, I was summoned to a classroom empty except for a row of young judges. They were seated and I stood there before them. One of them smiled. He it was who had found my animal antics so amusing in Xingtai that he laughed out loud. They ordered me to give them the notes.

The memory of that young man's smile still makes me shudder. Leonardo painted the famous smile of the Mona Lisa; who would want to paint a smile that makes men shudder? The smile of a Judas who delights in betraying his friend or murdering others?

Those little animal antics were a heavy cross, firmly nailed on. Finally I was released; but there were others who would never smile again. If only those scoundrels could have smiled with compassion, laughed like human beings instead of stirring up trouble and battening on others, like the beasts, reptiles and insects I drew.

Now here's an amazing thing. My notes disappeared after my meeting with my judges only to reappear once more, re-assembled by my friends from the big character posters pasted up denouncing me. Funnily, pieces by other writers, far better than mine, had been included. Sadly, since they were not mine, I have been forced to omit them from my collection. ❑

From the introduction to Animal Antics *(written 1964, revised 1983)*
Translated by Yang Xianyi

The donkey on the treadmill
*Running fast like this every day is so hard,
but where does it get me?*

The parrot
*I parrot everybody's words
but I've no idea what they mean*

The monkey
*No matter what a serious face I put on,
people still call me a monkey*

The dog
I've lost my master so I have to wag my tail at anyone I meet

The snail
Petit bourgeois! Me! Nonsense. You've no idea what fun it is to own your own home

The tiger
The phrase 'Paper Tiger'* has ruined my reputation: I'll have to change my name (*Mao's term for imperialists)

Huang Yongyu, *now living in Hong Kong, is one of the foremost living Chinese artists. He was forced to leave China in May 1989 after suggesting that Mao's body be cremated*

My sculpture

MY HOMETOWN wasn't on a grand scale, yet it had some 50 or 60 temples, large and small; I can still recall 28 or 29 of them. Now they've all gone, reduced to dust. Not destroyed out of spite, simply ignorance.

The road along the outside of the city wall, from the east gate to the south gate, was lined with workshops, all specialising in carving wooden images of the deities. Whenever I was cutting class — frequently — this was my place of pilgrimage. Everything I ever learnt about art I learned in that street, from countless teachers, not one of whose names I can remember today.

'I've heard there's a thing called freedom'

Though I began with wood-cuts — which I taught for several decades in the department of engraving at the Central Academy of Fine Arts in Beijing — and painting on paper, sculpture is what I like best; it is the simplest and most direct way of expressing ideas and what I have worked on most recently.

My 'Jesus' figure, with bullet holes in its chest, and the 'Hands of June', a group of dismembered hands severed by tank tracks, commemorate 4 June. 'Rumours', 'Teacher and model for all generations' and 'Leniency for those who confess their Crimes', along with two pieces inspired by the poetry of Shelley — 'Spring days not far away' and 'I've heard there's a thing called freedom' — were made in memory of the Cultural Revolution. In memory of the owl I painted for the Beijing Hotel, which became a target of [political] criticism in 1975, I made another owl, which was shown in my most recent exhibition.

I was 28 when I returned to Beijing, full of passion for the task of building the revolution; now I'm 74. The first time I marched in Tiananmen, as the great leader Chairman Mao looked on, hot tears streamed down my cheeks and I couldn't see the road in front of me. **HY**

MA JIAN

Citizen of the floating world

For the people of Hong Kong, 1 July 1997 means a transformation of identity: they become — Chinese citizens. I myself am a Chinese citizen. Since I emigrated to Hong Kong seven years ago, my sense of identity has changed, become blurred, but though I cannot say with the confidence of the Hong Kong native that: 'I am from Hong Kong', I can still say, 'I live in Hong Kong'. But from 1 July, the drift begins: Hong Kong becomes a floating island, migrating on the map.

When I arrived, seven years ago, at this island of safety, the customs post was like a wall blocking out the rays of despotic red light: I was safe, I was free. My field of vision and sense of time had changed, as though I had passed through a time tunnel. I looked at China as if it were the butt of time. Now that I live on a floating island, this vantage-point of mine has lost its sense of direction, of time.

As we watch, incredulously, pre-ordained history advances, or rather, steps backwards to meet us. No-one asks whether we accept the past, whether we can go and relive the time we have already lived. It is as though, studying at middle school, we are suddenly sent back to kindergarten.

The Chinese love their land and love their homes. But because their souls have been diminished, they have lost their dignity. They are not born with a sense of security. On the contrary, to be Chinese means to announce that you accept being controlled by someone else, that you forfeit a human's most basic needs and that you are estranged from your time and epoch.

In China, I was an artist. My enemies were clearly defined. From those in office, I demanded rights and freedom. It was like being on a battlefield, at any moment the sky might fall on your head. For these seven years in Hong Kong, I have remained an artist, but I have left the arena. My anger can no longer be seen from the outside, it remains in my heart, inside my body. As a fugitive, I have lost my terra firma. Girlfriends have left me, too, because our lifestyles were incompatible. I am a bad risk: behind me lies the landscape of socialism and they lose heart. Still, I will not leave Hong Kong. Someone who has been used to living in a prison is none too cheerfully optimistic about freedom in this life.

Ma Jian is a writer and photographer from Beijing now living in Hong Kong Translated by Oliver Kramer